The Power of a Mother's Prayer

*Changing Lives and Relationships
Through Heaven's Life Line
with the Holy Spirit*

Phillippa M. Turner

TEACH Services, Inc.
P U B L I S H I N G
www.TEACHServices.com • (800) 367-1844

World rights reserved. This book or any portion thereof may not be copied or reproduced in any form or manner whatever, except as provided by law, without the written permission of the publisher, except by a reviewer who may quote brief passages in a review.

The author assumes full responsibility for the accuracy of all facts and quotations as cited in this book. The opinions expressed in this book are the author's personal views and interpretations, and do not necessarily reflect those of the publisher.

This book is provided with the understanding that the publisher is not engaged in giving spiritual, legal, medical, or other professional advice. If authoritative advice is needed, the reader should seek the counsel of a competent professional.

Copyright © 2018 Phillippa M. Turner
Copyright © 2018 TEACH Services, Inc.
ISBN-13: 978-1-4796-0897-3 (Paperback)
ISBN-13: 978-1-4796-0898-0 (ePub)
Library of Congress Control Number: 2018943414

Unless otherwise indicated, all Scripture quotations are from the New King James Version® (NKJV), copyright © 1982 by Thomas Nelson. Used by permission. All rights reserved.

Published by

www.TEACHServices.com • (800) 367-1844

Table of Contents

Dedication .... *v*

Reviews .... *vii*

Introduction .... *xi*

1   The Agony of a Grieving Mom and an Incredible Conversation with God 15

2   Why Trials and Afflictions? 26

3   Here Am I, Send Me 39

4   Live! Live! Live! 48

5   Praying Moms International 55

6   A House of Prayer for All Nations 68

7   Learning Patience to be Patient 81

8   What is Intercessory Prayer? 89

9   Before You Call I Will Answer 109

10 The Family Power-Packed Prayer Line 118

11 Rejoice with Me! 134

Bibliography *147*

Dedication

I dedicate this book to the Holy Spirit. He led me on an amazing journey to discover the true meaning of prayer—an intimate relationship with God.

To Ayesha, my beloved only child. Because of her continued support and love throughout the writing of this book, and within my own life, she taught me how to love again, forgive more, and pray without ceasing.

To all parents, especially single mothers and fathers. If you have a broken relationship with your child, may this book give you hope.

Reviews

"***The Power of a Mother's Prayer*** has been a true blessing to me. Early in the book, I was able to sense the pain and anguish Sis. Turner experienced by the feeling of helplessness in dealing with her daughter. I can only imagine what it must have been like in the beginning, but being a mother of two myself, I understand the necessity of fervent and consistent prayer for your children. Sis. Turner pointed us to the precious promise of God regarding our children from the book *Education, pg. 18* by Ellen White: "Higher than the highest human thought can reach is God's ideal for His children." Without constant communion with Him, this goal cannot be reached.

Sis. Turner went to war with God to save her daughter's life and in the process, God revealed Himself to her in ways that had yet been unimagined. Even through personal tragedies, He taught her patience while shaping her and preparing her for an awesome ministry. What a magnificent testimony to the power of God as we submit in obedience to His will!

Out of a sincere and willing heart was birthed a powerful prayer ministry that has grown and spread to influence countless others for the cause of Christ. Sis. Turner was blessed by God, as reflected in the words of Isaiah 57:15 which states "For thus saith the high and lofty One that inhabiteth eternity, whose name is holy; I dwell in the high and holy place, with him [and her] also that is of a contrite and humble spirit, to revive the spirit of the humble, and to revive the heart of the contrite ones." Her humble and contrite spirit is what allowed the Holy Spirit to minister to her and show her more and more of His mighty power in her life.

From forming "Praying Mothers International" to inspiring the Southeastern Conference president to form a prayer ministries department to starting a vibrant prayer line, there is evidence of a deep sense of the presence of God is Sis. Turner's life. I am grateful to God for leading me to this powerful praying woman of God that has become a member of the Southeastern Conference prayer team. I had no prior knowledge of her or her ministry, except that God brought us together for such a time as this. May all the readers of this book be encouraged to develop a life of deep, consistent, and abiding prayer with our heavenly Father. He will not turn a deaf ear to the sincere heart, as evidenced by Psalms 66:19,20: "But verily God hath heard me; he hath attended to the voice of my prayer. Blessed be God, which hath not turned away my prayer, nor His mercy from me."

—**Mithra Williams**, Prayer and Women's Ministries Director
Southeastern Conference of Seventh-day Adventists

"For anyone who is in dire need of transformational answers to prayer, ***The Power of a Mother's Prayer*** is the book you've been waiting for. Following the leading of the Holy Spirit, the author takes you on wings of prayer into the deep treasure house of holy promises found in Scripture and the inspired works of Ellen G. White. To the persevering heart is made real the assurance that God really does hear and answer prayer."

—**Angelle Roberts**, Ph.D.

"As I read this book, it became evident that the author found herself in God's laboratory of teaching her the true meaning of intercessory prayer. Each chapter creates a desire to know what will be the outcome of this mother-daughter experience. As a pastor with over 30 years of pastoral ministry, I can truly say that *The Power of a Mother's Prayer* rates near the top from a lay member. The book is a very practical book on how one should thirst after God's presence and guidance through the challenges of life. I believe because the book is a play by play experience of how a mother sought God's guidance on saving her daughter, one can gather the practical tools needed to tackle any challenge one may face. As a mother fought to save her only child, she discovered her God given gift of intercessory prayer. The book also offers practical models to expand prayer ministries. Phillippa Turner shows us how she prays and through her experience helps us understand the how to of intercessory prayer.

This book inspired me to revisit intercessory prayer and also provided a guide to start a sustainable prayer ministry. The one practical aspect that gripped my attention was the chapter on "The Family Power-Packed Prayer Line." This chapter is God in action as a result of intercessory prayer. All I can say, is Wow! This is a must read for anyone seeking to understand the deeper things of how God never leaves you or forsakes you!"

—**Dr. Donald L. Burden**, Senior Pastor
Lighthouse 7th Day Adventist Church
Fort Lauderdale, Florida

"When the author made up her mind to allow God to fight her battles and began standing upon the promises of God, this allowed her prayer life to reach higher Heights and deeper depths. This author embarked upon and amazing journey and took her readers through what I would call a "Faith" walk. She endured hardship and conflicts with her only child, her daughter, and as a result the mother-daughter relationship slowly declined and eventually became disastrous. This Author called upon the name of the Lord and the miraculous began to unfold in the author's life.

After reading this amazing book, it has provided me with great insights into the heart of a praying mother. I too have a praying mother and this book has allowed me to truly understand and believe in the power of prayer and the heart of a desperate mother determined to intercede on her child's behalf. It expresses the perseverance and sacrifice that came through what this author endured. The scriptural references in this book provided great insights and reference points. This book speaks to the mothers who are still fighting, the teenager who may be searching for help, wanting and longing for that unconditional love of a mother. They can take comfort in knowing that God truly restores broken relationships. This book speaks to the faithless and the broken. This book will encourage the faithful to keep praying and fighting. Encourage, convict and empower the teenagers and adults who may have similar challenges in their households and lift the spirit of parents who are on the verge of giving up. This author highlighted several scriptures which will remind us of the Word of God and His promises for us. I recommend this book to all readers."

—**Keron Shand**, Social Worker, Young Adult Apostolic Pentecostal Faith

Introduction

> For I know the thoughts that I think toward you, says the
> LORD, thoughts of peace and not of evil, to give you a future
> and a hope. Then you will call upon Me and go and pray
> to Me, and I will listen to you. And you will seek Me and
> find Me, when you search for Me with all your heart.
> —Jeremiah 29:11–13

This is my personal journey in learning about the role of intercessory prayer, the power of God's Word to change lives, and the Holy Spirit's power to speak to the mind and convict and impress the heart with truth. This book was written not only from theoretical knowledge but also from my personal experience in hearing and obeying the voice of the Holy Spirit. The journey began when my gifted child was expelled from a prestigious, secular university pre-med program. My only hope was to surrender my life to God. I purposed in my heart to pray without ceasing for her salvation, and I began agonizing and pleading with God to save her. She had lost her faith and had plunged into a world of complete darkness with despair pressing heavily upon our souls as we tried to navigate and restore a broken mother-and-child relationship. We were in a crisis. Prayer was our only answer.

This book is not intended to be an exhaustive study of intercessory prayer and the Holy Spirit's transforming power. Rather, in it, readers will learn how God used this great crisis to transform my life from that of a nominal Christian to that of a real and practical Christian. They will also understand how God answers the prayers of a penitent, pleading, grieving, and humble mother.

My encounter with the Holy Spirit will enlighten readers about the importance of studying and searching the Scriptures daily. They will be captivated by the power and personality of the Holy Spirit. Jesus describes Him in John 16:13, 14: "However, when He, the Spirit of truth, has come, He will guide you into all truth; for He will not speak on His own authority, but whatever He hears He will speak; and He will tell you things to come. He will glorify Me, for He will take of what is Mine and declare it to you."

The Holy Spirit became my Guide, Counselor, Comforter, and Helper during this crisis. He taught me how to be patient during trials and afflictions. He impressed me how to pray, what to pray about, and when to pray.

Paul introduces the Holy Spirit as a Helper. "Likewise the Spirit also helps in our weaknesses. For we do not know what we should pray for as we ought, but the Spirit Himself makes intercession for us with groanings which cannot be uttered" (Rom. 8:26).

Join me in meeting the Holy Spirit and witnessing how He immersed me in the presence of God so that I radiated His grace and mercy to my daughter, becoming a powerful witness to her. Observe how He allowed me to encourage other parents whose children had left the church or were expelled from college or university.

The incredible stories of God's intervention in my life and my daughter's life will excite you as you read. You will be thrilled by the amazing transformation in our lives when I dared to pray. The Scriptures will come alive by my testimony. God answered all my prayers specifically with scripture. Not all the answers were pleasant. Nevertheless, they were lifesaving. For example, He reminded me in Ephesians 4:29, "Let no corrupt word proceed out of your mouth, but what is good for necessary edification, that it may impart grace to the hearers." In Psalm 39:1, He emphasized the principle, "I will guard my ways, lest I sin with my tongue; I will restrain my mouth with a muzzle." And, in Ecclesiastes 5:2, He told me how to guard my ways, "Do not be rash with your mouth, and let not your heart utter anything hastily before God. For God is in heaven, and you on earth; therefore let your words be few" (Eccles. 5:2). These scriptural words of advice changed my perspective in dealing with my daughter and with friends, staff, and anyone else I dealt with.

Come with me on this remarkable, wonderful, fulfilling journey and experience God's sovereignty as you recognize that He has total control of all things in our lives. He knows our past, our present, and our future. Nothing that has happened in our lives is beyond His knowledge or control. As the sovereign of the universe, He has done according to His will in our lives. He has transformed our lives of darkness into the splendor of His glorious light.

> **As the sovereign of the universe, He has done according to His will in our lives.**

The sovereign God declared to me in Isaiah 46:9: "I am God, and there is none like me." In Isaiah 48:10, 11, He reminded me of the reason He allowed me to experience trials and afflictions. "Behold, I have refined you, but not as silver. I have tested you in the furnace of affliction. For My sake, for My own sake, I will do it.... and I will not give My glory to another." He knows our past, our present, and our future. These texts confirm this knowledge. "Declaring the end from the beginning, and from ancient times things that are not yet done, saying, 'My counsel shall stand, and I will do all My pleasure'" (Isa. 46:10). "I know that You can do everything, and that no purpose of Yours can be withheld from You" (Job 42:2). "O LORD God of our fathers, are You not God in heaven, and do You not rule over all the kingdoms of the nations, and in Your hand is there not power and might, so that no one is able to withstand?" (2 Chron. 20:6).

"O taste and see that the Lord is good, blessed is the man who trusts in Him!" (Ps. 34:8). Taste and see how the Lord has been extraordinarily good to my daughter. The Holy Spirit worked behind the scenes like the moving of the wind. He brought life back to my spiritually dead daughter. Hear what He said about her while she was refusing to speak to me. I prayed, and He reminded me: "It is the Spirit who gives life; the flesh profits nothing. The words that I speak to you are spirit, and they are life" (John 6:63).

Be blessed as you embark on this Spirit-filled journey of God's power to change lives. He gave this promise to me during the crisis, a promise that has been fulfilled in our lives: "Then I will sprinkle clean water on you, and you shall be clean; I will cleanse you from all your filthiness and from all your idols. I will give you a new heart and put a new spirit within you; I will take the heart of stone out of your flesh and give you a heart of flesh. I will put My Spirit within you and cause you to walk in My statutes, and you will keep My judgments and do them" (Ezek. 37:25–27).

CHAPTER 1

The Agony of a Grieving Mom and an Incredible Conversation with God

> Arise, cry out in the night, At the beginning of the watches;
> Pour out your heart like water before the face of the Lord.
> Lift your hands toward Him For the life of your young
> children, who faint from hunger at the head of every street.
> —Lamentations 2:19

Satan has set up his kingdom on this earth, and he would like to claim our sons and daughters as his own. He allures and tempts them to follow him instead of God. He takes them captive and makes them slaves to his schemes. He was successful in targeting and entrapping my child. His temptations and allurements resulted in her expulsion from the university.

Satan is not concerned about who he tempts. He even tempted the Son of God. Matthew chapter four records the temptations of Jesus. Through the Word, Jesus was able to overcome Satan's temptations. He was a student of the Scriptures. At the very tender age of twelve, He baffled the priests in the temple. They were confounded by His knowledge of the Scriptures.

When Jesus was a young man, but prior to His call to fulfill His ministry, Satan tried to stop the plan of salvation. He tried to tempt Jesus by promising Him anything He wanted if He would worship Satan. Jesus reminded Satan, "It is written again, 'You shall not tempt the LORD your God'" (Matt. 4:7). Jesus overcame Satan in the wilderness and gained an even greater victory at the cross.

My daughter and the children of many other Christians are defenseless against Satan's attacks because they do not study the Scriptures. They are powerless against temptation and incapable of giving a defense for their faith. Paul wrote Timothy, who was then a young man: "Study to shew thyself approved unto God, a workman that needeth not to be ashamed, rightly dividing the word of truth" (2 Tim. 2:15, KJV). Peter encouraged his readers, "But sanctify the Lord God in your hearts, and always be ready to give a defense to everyone who asks you a reason for the hope that is in you, with meekness and fear" (1 Peter 3:15).

My daughter had not developed a knowledge of God's Word, nor did she trust in God's promises, as in Isaiah 40:29-31, which says: "He gives power to the weak, and to those who have no might He increases strength. Even the youths shall faint and be weary, and the young men shall utterly fall, but those who wait on the LORD shall renew their strength; they shall mount up with wings like eagles, they shall run and not be weary, they shall walk and not faint." My daughter did not know the strength that Ellen White proclaimed. "The enemy never can take out of the hand of Christ the one who is simply trusting in His promises" (Ms. 92, 1901, in *The Seventh-day Adventist Bible Commentary*, vol. 7, p. 959).

Satan was successful in targeting and entrapping my child. He attempted to take her out of God's hands. The temptations were alluring, and her succumbing to them resulted in her expulsion from the university for poor academic performance, though she had shown herself to be a gifted honor student.

Though discouraged and disappointed, I held on to the promise that God would never leave me nor forsake either my daughter or me, as Paul wrote: "Who shall separate us from the love of Christ? shall tribulation, or distress, or persecution, or famine, or nakedness, or peril or sword? As it is written: 'For Your sake we are killed all day long; we are accounted as sheep for the slaughter.' Yet in all these things we are more than conquerors through Him who loved us. For I am persuaded that neither death nor life, nor angels nor principalities nor powers, nor things present nor things to come, nor height nor depth, nor any other created thing, shall be able to separate us from the love of God which is in Christ Jesus our Lord" (Rom. 8:35–39). I was also comforted by the inspired words of Ellen White, "Instead of thinking of your discouragements, think of the power you can claim in Christ's name. Let your imagination take hold upon things unseen. Let your thoughts be directed to the great evidences of the great love of God for you. Faith can endure trial, resist temptation, bear up under disappointment. Jesus lives as our advocate. All is ours that His mediation secures.… All experiences and circumstances are God's workmen whereby good is brought to us" (*The Ministry of Healing*, p. 488).

I prayed tearfully and passionately for the Lord to redeem her from the hands of Satan. He consoled me with these words: "But now, thus says the LORD, who created you, O Jacob, And He who formed you, O Israel: 'Fear not, for I have redeemed you; I have called you by your name; You are Mine. When you pass through the waters, I will be with you; And through the rivers, they shall not overflow you. When you walk through the fire, you shall not be burned, nor shall the flame scorch you.

For I am the LORD your God, The Holy One of Israel, your Savior; I gave Egypt for your ransom, Ethiopia and Seba in your place'" (Isa. 43:1–3).

At eighteen years of age, my daughter's inability to comprehend being separated from her friends and from the university that she had come to cherish left her broken and confused. She felt abandoned by God and by her friends and family, and she took out her bitterness and wrath on me.

I cried out to the Lord as the psalmist advised me: "Call upon Me in the day of trouble; I will deliver you, and you shall glorify Me" (Ps. 50:15).

Angrily I asked the Lord, "How will I honor and glorify You when I am in this furnace of affliction and disappointment and the object of my daughter's bitterness?"

He reminded me through His servant Ellen White: "God has always tried His people in the furnace of affliction. It is in the heat of the furnace that the dross is separated from the true gold of the Christian character. Jesus watches the test; He knows what is needed to purify the precious metal, that it may reflect the radiance of His love. It is by close, testing trials that God disciplines His servants.... He shows them their own weakness, and teaches them to lean upon Him; for He is their only help and safeguard. Thus His object is attained. They are educated, trained, and disciplined, prepared to fulfill the grand purpose for which their powers were given them. When God calls them to action, they are ready, and heavenly angels can unite with them in the work to be accomplished on earth" (*Patriarchs and Prophets*, pp. 129, 130).

"How will You show me my own weakness in dealing with my daughter?" I prayed.

"This will be revealed when you seek Me with all your might" was the Lord's response.

The prophet Jeremiah described the process in his book: "Then you will call upon Me and go and pray to Me, and I will listen to you. And you shall seek Me and find Me, when you search for Me with all your heart" (Jer. 29:12, 13).

"How will You teach me to lean on You that I may reflect the radiance of Your love to my daughter?" I said.

"Pray and keep on praying," was His response.

I agonized with the Lord, praying, fasting, and studying His Word for the salvation of my child (something I still do). In the following comment, Ellen White confirms God's answer to a mother's prayers: "The prayers of Christian mothers are not disregarded by the Father of all, who sent His Son to the earth to ransom a people for Himself. He will not turn away your petitions and leave you and yours to the buffetings of Satan in the great day of final conflict. It is for you to work with simplicity and faithfulness, and God will establish the work of your hands" (*Child Guidance*, p. 526).

God did not turn away from my daughter or leave her to the buffeting of Satan. As I begged the Lord to save and redeem her, I observed that she experienced extraordinary changes in her life. It was remarkable to see how the Holy Spirit transformed her life daily in small but noticeable ways. She wrote in my birthday card, "I am so blessed to have you as my mother," though, during our crisis, she had remarked, "I will never have a relationship with you." The power of prayer heals all broken heart and wounds.

The words of the prophet Ezekiel confirmed the prayer I lifted daily for my daughter and me. "I will give you a new heart and put a new spirit within you; I will take the heart of stone out of your flesh and give you a heart of flesh" (Ezek. 36:26).

On the day of Pentecost, Peter told the people, "Repent, and let every one of you be baptized in the name of Jesus Christ for the remission of sins; and you shall receive the gift of the Holy Spirit. For the promise is to you and to your children, and to all who are afar off, as many as the Lord our God will call" (Acts 2:39). I have repented for myself and for my daughter, and I have asked God to forgive us.

The promised new heart was made manifest in a change in her behavior and mine. Her willingness to be courteous and civil to me and to other family members was evidence that the change was taking place. Daily I witnessed the evidence of the Holy Spirit's working in our lives. This was an amazing blessing in my own Christian experience. It helped me develop a better relationship with God and with my daughter. I continued to pray and read my Bible more often. I gained the victory over anger, disappointment, pain, and the desire to fix my daughter's life immediately.

My faith increased daily as I prevailed and persevered in prayer for my salvation and that of my daughter. Like Jacob, I refused to give up. Jacob wrestled with the Lord until the Lord blessed him. He gained the victory because he prayed. I desired the Lord's blessing so that my child could see Christ in me.

I said, "Father, I will not stop praying for myself or my daughter until you bless us."

He answered me immediately through Matthew 7:7, confirming my prayer by saying, "Ask, and it will be given to you; seek, and you shall find; knock, and it will be opened to you."

I was encouraged by Ellen White's reflection on Jacob's prevailing prayer. "Jacob prevailed because he was persevering and determined. His experience testifies to the power of importunate prayer. It is now that we are to learn this lesson of prevailing prayer, of unyielding faith. The greatest victories to the church of Christ or to the individual Christian are not those that are gained by talent or education, by wealth or the favor of men. They are those victories that are gained in the audience chamber with God, when earnest, agonizing faith lays hold upon the mighty arm of power. Those who are unwilling to forsake every sin and to seek earnestly for God's blessing, will not obtain it. But all who will lay hold of God's promises as did Jacob, and be as earnest and persevering as he was, will succeed as he succeeded. 'Shall not God avenge His own elect, which cry day and night to Him, though He bear long with them?' Luke 18:7, 8" (*Patriarchs and Prophets*, p. 203).

The Holy Spirit made a strong impression on my mind, and an incredible, almost audible conversation took place. With unspeakable awe, I heard Him instruct me:

"Tell mothers about your remarkable experience and the power of God when you pray. Let them know that I allowed you to endure trials and afflictions so you could comfort others who are going through similar experiences with their children. Tell them that trials are God's method of training for success and that there is value in suffering."

"You mean me?" I answered.

"Yes," was His reply.

"Assure parents that there is hope for their children if they will 'pray without ceasing' (1 Thess. 5:17). Tell them how Satan tried to rob you of your intimacy with Me by attempting to destroy your daughter's life. Point out how you supplicated Me in your distress and how I always answered your prayers from the Scriptures. Explain to them why I told you to search and read the Scriptures daily."

> **The Holy Spirit made a strong impression on my mind, and an incredible, almost audible conversation took place.**

Jesus said: "You search the Scriptures, for in them you think you have eternal life; and these are they which testify of Me" (John 5:39).

There was more.

"Inform them that one night, in your agony and pain, you prostrated yourself and buried your face in the carpet. You wept bitterly and prayed with inarticulate groans, and I answered with the wonderful promise, 'I have heard your prayer, I have seen your tears … I will deliver you' (Isa. 38:5, 6). Let them know that, although your daughter has not fully accepted the Lord, I have promised you in Luke, chapter 15, that she will be saved."

Luke, chapter 15, deals with the parables of the lost sheep, the lost coin, and the prodigal son. The chapter could be titled, "The Lost Are

Found Because of God's Amazing Grace." These parables bring out, in different ways, God's redemptive power for those who have strayed from Him. They illustrate that, although our children may have turned from God, He does not leave them to the command of Satan with its misery. He is kind and loving to all who are exposed to Satan's tricks. The parable of the prodigal son deals with those who have known the Father's love but have allowed Satan to make them captive at his will. However, through God's intervention, the prodigal returns home safely.

The second parable demonstrates how God takes the initiative to seek and find even one sheep out of a hundred that is lost. He finds that sheep and brings it back to the fold. Then He rejoices that the wandering one is safely back home.

The third parable shows God's amazing power in seeking the lost. Jesus asked the following question: "What woman, having ten silver coins, if she loses one coin, does not light a lamp, sweep the house, and search carefully until she finds it?" (Luke 15:8).

I had my own single piece of silver—my only child. She was lost in sin within my house. To find her, my lamp—my life—needed to be lighted. My house needed to be swept diligently until she was found. I needed to seek through prayer God's amazing power to heal and restore.

Ellen White confirmed the meaning of the story: "This parable has a lesson to families. In the household there is often great carelessness concerning the souls of its members. Among their number may be one who is estranged from God; but how little anxiety is felt lest in the family relationship there be lost one of God's entrusted gifts. The coin, though lying among dust and rubbish, is a piece of silver still. Its owner seeks it because it is of value. So every soul, however degraded by sin, is in God's sight accounted precious.... So in the family if one member is lost to God every means should be used for his recovery" (*Christ Object Lessons*, p. 194).

"What means should I use in her recovery?" I asked the Holy Spirit.

"Your influence in her life," was the response.

I recognized that my influence for good or evil would be the best way for me to reach her and save her. I knew that I needed to practice practical Christianity. I purposed in my heart to be a blessing in word and actions. The apostle Paul reminds us: "For we are to God the fragrance of Christ among those who are being saved and among those who are perishing. To the one we are the aroma of death leading to death, and to the other the aroma of life leading to life. And who is sufficient for these things?" (2 Cor. 2:15, 16).

The thought that my life could mean either life or death to my daughter was sobering and fearful. I asked the Holy Spirit to fill me daily so that I could be a sweet-smelling fragrance to influence her positively.

One day in this process, without discussion, she exclaimed, "Mom, I love you. Thank you for all you have done for me." Ellen White called attention to the power of influence:

> That our influence should be a savor of death unto death is a fearful thought, yet it is possible. One soul misled, forfeiting eternal bliss—who can estimate the loss? And yet one rash act, one thoughtless word, on our part may exert so deep an influence on the life of another that it will prove the ruin of his soul. One blemish on the character may turn many away from Christ.
>
> As the seed sown produces a harvest, and this in turn is sown, the harvest is multiplied. In our relation to others, this law holds true. Every act, every word, is a seed that will bear fruit. Every deed of thoughtful kindness, of obedience, of self-denial, will reproduce itself in others, and through them in still others. So every act of envy, malice, or dissension is a seed that will spring up in a "root of bitterness" whereby many shall be defiled. Hebrews 12:15. And how much larger number will the "many" poison! Thus the sowing of good and evil goes on for time and for eternity. (*Prophets and Kings*, p. 86)

The Holy Spirit influenced her life. She acknowledged that she felt my prayers in her life and told her friends about her praying mother. They began to call to request that I pray with and for them. A seed was sown. The harvest multiplied. Lives were blessed because I allowed the Holy Spirit to allow me to be a positive influence on my daughter.

I continued to demonstrate love and patience and to exert a positive influence on her.

"What else should I know about this parable?" I asked the Holy Spirit.

"You are the woman who represents Christ in this parable. You must act just as Christ acted towards those who opposed Him. Search for your daughter diligently. With My blessing, she will be found.

"And when she has found it, she calls her friends and neighbors together, saying, 'Rejoice with me, for I have found the piece which I lost!' Likewise, I say to you, there is joy in the presence of the angels of God over one sinner who repents" (Luke 15:9, 10).

With the consciousness of being in the presence of the holy, compassionate, merciful God, I continued praying, and He continued holding this incredible conversation with me.

"Articulate for parents how you prayed earnestly and how I confirmed your prayers with specific promises from the Word."

Note Ellen White's inspired comments about God's promises.

> We should now acquaint ourselves with God by proving His promises. Angels record every prayer that is earnest and sincere. We should rather dispense with selfish gratifications than neglect communion with God. The deepest poverty, the greatest self-denial, with His approval, is better than riches, honors, ease, and friendship without it. We must take time to pray. If we allow our minds to be absorbed by worldly interests, the Lord may give us time by removing from us our idols of gold, of houses, or of fertile lands. (*The Great Controversy*, p. 622)

The Holy Spirit told me: "Inform them how the promises of God became real to you." He promised, "You will show me the path of life; in Your presence is fullness of joy; at Your right hand are pleasures of joy forever more" (Ps. 16:11).

I hesitated. "How will I educate mothers about your goodness and mercy towards me and my daughter?"

The Holy Spirit responded, "Form a prayer group for mothers."

This astonishing conversation and the possibility of my only child losing her salvation compelled me to start the prayer group "Praying Moms International."

CHAPTER 2

Why Trials and Afflictions?

> Beloved, do not think it strange concerning the fiery trial
> which is to try you, as though some strange thing happened
> to you; but rejoice to the extent that you partake of
> Christ's sufferings, that when His glory is revealed,
> you may also be glad with exceeding joy.
> —1 Peter 4:12, 13

"Why me Lord? Why did you allow my gifted daughter to be expelled from the university? What have I done to deserve this? And why now? It is my turn to be free—free from the stress of being a single mother. What will family, friends, and church members say about me? All my friends' children are successful. What will they say about you, God? Where are you when I need you?"

Confronted with the severest challenge of my life, I demanded that God answer these questions. At the end of her freshman year, my gifted eighteen-year-old had been expelled from a prestigious secular university pre-med program.

My child, a most precious and beloved daughter, returned home. She was broken, and my home became a war zone, which had never been our intention. However, Satan, the accuser and deceiver, gained entrance into our home by inserting himself into our daily activities. Our home was embattled with the severest trial, suffering, and affliction.

To understand what was happening, I asked the Holy Spirit the following questions:

"What is a trial and affliction? And why am I experiencing this trial now?"

He directed me to the Merriam-Webster dictionary, which defined the word "trial" as "a test of faith, patience, or stamina through subjection to suffering or temptation: broadly: a source of vexation or annoyance."

"How is affliction different from trial?" I asked.

Dictionary.com defines "affliction" as "a state of pain, distress, or grief: misery." Thus, affliction refers to an event or circumstance that is hard to bear. Affliction is also defined as a state of pain, distress, grief, or misery that lies deep in the soul. It is usually associated with deep loss of something most dear, whether friends, relatives, or health. These answers allowed me to develop a strategy to combat Satan's attempts to use my child to disrupt God's plan for our lives on our journey to His kingdom. Until I allowed the Lord to take control and lead us through this storm, it seemed to be a long perilous journey. At the end of the storm is a rainbow. I eagerly anticipated *my* rainbow.

> **At the end of the storm is a rainbow. I eagerly anticipated *my* rainbow.**

Yet, God's Word is very sure. The Holy Spirit reminded me in Zephaniah 3:17: "The LORD your God in your midst, The Mighty One, will save; He will rejoice over you with gladness, He will quiet you with His love, He will rejoice over you with singing." I also considered Ellen White's encouragement, "Amidst the deepening shadows of earth's last great crisis, God's light will shine brightest, and the song of hope and trust will be heard in clearest and loftiest strain" (*Education*, p. 166).

In my distress, God was singing and rejoicing over me, cheering me on as I took this journey of trial and afflictions. He reminded me in Isaiah 54:17: "No weapon formed against you shall prosper, and every tongue which rises against you in judgment you shall condemn." I remembered again Ellen White's encouragement regarding the outcome of these trials, for she said that they would end with singing and rejoicing.

The Bible teaches that all Christians are to experience suffering that will severely test their faith. My faith was being severely tested. I almost gave up on God. However, I remembered that the Bible also teaches that trials are not an indicator of my faith or lack thereof, but, rather, they are tools used by God for His purposes, all of which benefit us and bring glory to His name and lead us to enjoy His goodness forever. The apostle Paul reminded me in Romans 8:18 and 28: "For I consider that the sufferings of this present time are not worthy to be compared with the glory which shall be revealed in us.... And we know that all things work together for good to those who love God, to those who are the called according to His purpose."

I asked the Spirit: "Does God want to use my trials to bring glory to His name? Does He want to prepare me for the glory which will be revealed to me if I am faithful?"

I received a resounding answer after I prayed. "Behold, I have refined you, but not as silver; I have tested you in the furnace of affliction. For My own sake, for My own sake, I will do it; ... and I will not give My glory to another" (Isa. 48:10, 11).

To glorify God, my life should reflect—as much as possible—His perfect character, His moral excellence, His compassion, and His love for a world that is full of trials and afflictions. That very glory is given to all of us if we accept God's offer in prayer. I decided to trust God. I spent more time praying over the conflicts in our home. I discovered that there is power in prayer. More than anything, I wanted my voice to reach the ear of God.

Ellen White emphasized the real power that comes to us through prayer—

> The glory that rested upon Christ is a pledge of the love of God for us. It tells us of the power of prayer,—how the human voice may reach the ear of God, and our petitions find acceptance in the courts of heaven. By sin, earth was cut off from heaven, and alienated from its communion; but Jesus has connected it again with the sphere of glory. His love has encircled man, and reached the highest heaven. The light which fell from the open portals upon the head of our Saviour will fall upon us as we pray for help to resist temptation. The voice which spoke to Jesus says to every believing soul, This is My beloved child, in whom I am well pleased. (*The Desire of Ages*, p. 113)

I prayed: "Is God well pleased with me? Does He see something in me that He wants to purify for His glory? Has He chosen the method of trials, suffering, and affliction to purify my life for His service and glory?"

His wise response came through Ellen White's statement: "Trials and obstacles are the Lord's chosen methods of discipline and His appointed conditions of success. He who reads the hearts of men knows their characters better than they themselves know them. He sees that some have powers and susceptibilities which, rightly directed, might be used in the advancement of His work. In His providence He brings these persons into different positions and varied circumstances that they may discover in their character the defects which have been concealed from their own knowledge. He gives them opportunity to correct these defects and to fit themselves for His service. Often He permits the fires of affliction to assail them that they may be purified" (*The Ministry of Healing*, p. 471).

The Bible identifies reasons that God allows us to endure suffering, trials, and afflictions. Here is a partial list of these:

- **We suffer because we live in a fallen world.**

That there is a great controversy being waged between Christ and Satan is the reason that suffering exists in this world. Yet, God wants to reclaim us, while Satan wants to condemn us to cause us to lose our salvation. God, our Father, disciplines us because He loves us. Hebrews 12:6 declares: "For whom the Lord loves He chastens, and scourges every son whom He receives." Ellen White described the world before sin:

Before the entrance of evil there was peace and joy throughout the universe. All was in perfect harmony with the Creator's will. Love for God was supreme, love for one another impartial (*The Great Controversy*, p. 493).

The law of love is the foundation of God's government. All happiness for God's creatures depends on that great principle. God has given all intelligent beings the freedom of choice. However, there was one being who perverted that choice, becoming the originator of sin. He hated the law of love, which provided for perfect accord and harmony. His name was "Lucifer." Because he chose to break the perfect accord of love and harmony, he was kicked out of heaven. However, before he left, he corrupted one third of the angels. They too were kicked out of heaven and came to this earth where they continued their discord, infecting earth with sin.

- **Sometimes we suffer because of our own foolishness.**

The Bible tells us, in Galatians 6:7: "Do not be deceived, God is not mocked; for whatever a man sows, that he shall also reap." I reaped exactly what I had sowed. I am convinced that, had I not violated God's commandment and left the church, God in His wisdom would have provided me a godly husband. However, I chose to leave the church, and I had a child out of wedlock. I was a very foolish young woman. In leaving, I followed my own principles. Nonetheless, God did not leave me. He sent many people into my life to encourage me to get back on the right path. Ellen White's writing was instrumental in this journey, teaching me the practical lesson of why we suffer. In her analogy about the caged bird that sings she wrote:

> In the full light of day, and in hearing of the music of other voices, the caged bird will not sing the song that his master seeks to teach him. He learns a snatch of this, a trill of that, but never a separate and entire melody. But the master covers the cage, and places it where the bird will listen to the one song he is to sing. In the dark, he tries and tries again to sing that song until it is learned, and he breaks forth in perfect melody. Then the bird is brought forth, and ever after he can sing that song in the light. Thus God deals with His children. He has a song to teach us, and when we have learned it amid the shadows of affliction we can sing it ever afterward. (*The Ministry of Healing*, p. 472)

The trials and afflictions in my life have been the most valuable experiences of my spiritual journey. I have learned and applied lessons about love, patience, forgiveness, and compassion, and I have shared what I have learned with those I have met.

- **The Lord sometimes allows us to suffer so that we can help and strengthen others.**

The Lord allowed me to endure these trials with my daughter so that I could help and strengthen other mothers and relatives who have been experiencing similar problems. The Scriptures were my guide during this period of my life. Now I live and breathe the Word.

"'Comfort, yes, comfort My people!' says your God" (Isa. 40:1). I am happy that God comforts and answers prayers. Jesus, God's Son, placed me on His personal prayer list. "And the Lord said, "Simon, Simon! [or, in my case, Phillippa, Phillippa!] Indeed, Satan has asked for you, that he may sift you as wheat. But I have prayed for you, that your faith should not fail; and when you have returned to Me, strengthen your brethren" (Luke 22:31, 32). The Lord allowed me to strengthen others by forming "Praying Moms International" and by praying over thousands of prayer requests yearly as a 3ABN prayer warrior.

I also participate in the World Church United Prayer. I pray over weekly prayer requests from the General Conference of Seventh-day Adventists. The Lord also used me in relaying a message to the president of the Southeastern Conference of Seventh-day Adventists that he should start a prayer ministry. The prayer coordinator appointed me as one of the field prayer coordinators overseeing thirty churches. My responsibilities involve promoting the conference's and the General Conference's prayer initiative, in order for us to be a praying conference. I am privileged to also be the prayer coordinator of my local church Lighthouse Seventh-day Adventist Church.

Ellen White expands on this thought. "Those who have borne the greatest sorrows are frequently the ones who carry the greatest comfort to others, bringing sunshine wherever they go. Such ones have been chastened and sweetened by their afflictions; they did not lose confidence in God when trouble assailed them, but clung closer to His protecting love. Such ones are living proof of the tender care of God, who makes the darkness as well as the light and chastens us for our good" (*God's Amazing Grace*, p. 122).

- **Suffering brings us closer to God.**

James wrote: "Draw near to God and He will draw near to you" (James 4:8). The crisis with my daughter drew me into an intimate relationship with the Lord. When my days and nights were filled with sorrow and tears, God was the only answer for me. I am still clinging to Him. "Seek the LORD while He may be found, call upon Him while He is near. Let the wicked forsake his way, and the unrighteous man his thoughts; let him return to the LORD, and He will have mercy on him; and to our God, for He will abundantly pardon" (Isa. 55:6, 7). "The LORD is near to all who call upon Him, to all who call upon Him in truth" (Ps. 145:18). He is still my refuge and strong tower, a present help in my time of trouble. I was purified and strengthen through my trials. Ellen White brings this out further.

> Many of your afflictions have been visited upon you, in the wisdom of God, to bring you closer to the throne of grace. He softens and subdues His children by sorrows and trials. This world is God's workshop, where He fashions us for the courts of heaven. He uses the planing knife upon our quivering hearts until the roughness and irregularities are removed and we are fitted for our proper places in the heavenly building. Through tribulation and distress the Christian becomes purified and strengthened, and develops a character after the model that Christ has given. (*God's Amazing Grace*, p. 89)

Ellen White reminds us: "The very trials that task our faith most severely and make it seem that God has forsaken us, are to lead us closer to Christ, that we may lay all our burdens at His feet and experience the peace which He will give us in exchange" (*Patriarchs and Prophets*, p. 129).

- **Trials are a part of my education for serving the Lord.**

"How am I to learn God's plan for my life?" I inquired.

The Holy Spirit answered me with Psalm 32:8: "I will instruct you and teach you in the way you should go; I will guide you with My eye."

Mrs. White affirms: "Trial is part of the education given in the school of Christ, to purify God's children from the dross of earthliness" (*Acts of the Apostles*, p. 524).

Christ Himself entered the school of affliction. Paul states in Hebrews 5:8: "Though He was a Son, yet He learned obedience by the things which

He suffered." His example in learning the meaning of suffering is to help us understand why *we* suffer.

> "Trial is part of the education given in the school of Christ, to purify God's children from the dross of earthliness."

"But He was wounded for our transgressions, He was bruised for our iniquities; the chastisement for our peace was upon Him, and by His stripes we are healed. All we like sheep have gone astray; we have turned, every one, to his own way; and the LORD has laid on Him the iniquity of us all. He was oppressed and He was afflicted, yet He opened not His mouth; He was led as a lamb to the slaughter, and as a sheep before its shearers is silent, so He opened not His mouth" (Isa. 53:5–7). Because He suffered, He is able to teach us that, through the school of affliction, we can learn valuable lessons.

In Romans 5:3–8, Paul gives a most important reason for this education. It is for our hope and salvation. "And not only that, but we also glory in tribulations, knowing that tribulation produces perseverance; and perseverance, character; and character, hope. Now hope does not disappoint, because the love of God has been poured out in our hearts by the Holy Spirit who was given to us. For when we were still without strength, in due time Christ died for the ungodly. For scarcely for a righteous man will one die; yet perhaps for a good man someone would even dare to die. But God demonstrates His own love toward us, in that while we were still sinners, Christ died for us."

The lessons of love, forgiveness, humility, and kindness that I learned during my trials and tribulations have been invaluable to me in my journey to the kingdom. I have learned that my suffering was indeed a gift of grace, as Paul declared in Philippians 1:29: "For to you it has been granted on behalf of Christ, not only to believe in Him, but also to suffer for His sake." We suffer for Christ because of our faith. Mrs. White concurred.

"The trial of faith is more precious than gold. All should learn that this is a part of the discipline in the school of Christ, which is essential to purify and refine them from the dross of earthliness" (*God's Amazing Grace*, p. 81).

While my trials were severe, harsh, and painful, they were a tremendous learning experience and blessing to me. During one very heated conversation with my daughter, the Holy Spirit warned me:

"Do not say a word to her."

I was shocked by the command and repeated the command in a question.

"Do you mean that I should not say a word to her, even with the abusive way that she has been speaking to me?"

"Do not say a word," was the response. I obeyed the voice, and the yelling ceased. Calm and tranquility pervaded the house. I was immediately impressed by the Holy Spirit with the truth of Proverbs 15:1: "A soft answer turns away wrath, but a harsh word stirs up anger." Ellen White added this wise counsel:

> God in His great love is seeking to develop in us the precious graces of His Spirit. He permits us to encounter obstacles, persecution, and hardships, not as a curse, but as the greatest blessing of our lives. Every temptation resisted, every trial bravely borne, gives us a new experience and advances us in the work of character building. The soul that through divine power resists temptation reveals to the world and to the heavenly universe the efficiency of the grace of Christ. (*Thoughts from the Mount of Blessings*, p. 117)

I can only say, "Thank You, Holy Spirit" The discipline of following the instruction of the Holy Spirit was the greatest lesson and blessing during those tumultuous years and the turning point of healing in our relationship. I resisted the temptation to unleash my fury at her with bitter, sarcastic, and biting words. Instead, I showed her grace. God in His divine providence used that heated argument to teach me patience and to bring out something special He desired to develop in me. I transferred this instruction to my professional life. As a nursing supervisor, managers and staff meetings were boisterous at times. Whenever someone spoke harshly to me or about me, the phrase, "Do not say a word," echoed in my head. During heated discussions, I allowed the staff to vent their frustrations. Sometimes the concerns were not relevant to the meeting, yet I would listen and schedule a meeting with the staff that had the issues unrelated to the meeting. After listening, I discovered that the outburst in the meeting was from an unresolved conflict at home. The staff would apologize, and I would pray and ask God to bless them and resolve the personal issue.

As my trials and afflictions intensified, I continue to question God's motive.

"Why are you allowing these severe trials in my life? Why can't You use other means?"

Silence.

I resigned myself to continue the journey without any more murmuring. The Holy Spirit instructed me that the Lord was calling me to His service.

- **We suffer because God sees evidence of something valuable in us.**

I consoled myself, and I prayed. If God is permitting these trials, then the Bible must have the answers. I studied the Bible with intensity for inspiration and for a revelation that would answer my perplexing questions.

Isaiah 48:10 declares, "Behold, I have refined you, but not as silver; I have tested you in the furnace of affliction." The refining process was intense. Ellen White wrote:

> The fact that we are called upon to endure trial shows that the Lord Jesus sees in us something precious which He desires to

develop. If He saw in us nothing whereby He might glorify His name, He would not spend time in refining us. He does not cast worthless stones into His furnace. It is valuable ore that He refines. The blacksmith puts the iron and steel into the fire that he may know what manner of metal they are. The Lord allows His chosen ones to be placed in the furnace of affliction to prove what temper they are of and whether they can be fashioned for His work. (*The Ministry of Healing*, p. 471)

As the trials intensified, I continued to pray with specificity and intensity. Because God speaks directly to those who listen to His voice when they pray and read His Word, I asked the Holy Spirit to please answer all my prayers by means of Scripture, and He did. I marveled at the direct answers He gave me in response to my prayer requests. My faith was strengthened. Prayer became my passion.

Consider Ellen White's insightful comments: "The Bible is God's voice speaking to us, just as surely as though we could hear it with our ears" (*Testimonies for the Church*, vol. 6, p. 393). "The Scriptures are to be received as God's word to us, not written merely, but spoken.... In them He is speaking to us individually, speaking as directly as if we could listen to His voice" (*The Ministry of Healing*, p. 122).

And, yes, God spoke to me directly! All the Bible verses in this book were given to me either while I was praying or just after I had prayed. I learned to listen and wait for God to speak to me.

Here is a short list of the scriptures that God gave me about my affliction because I dared to pray and ask for scriptural confirmation.

"Many are the afflictions of the righteous, but the LORD delivers him out of them all" (Ps. 34:19).

"Before I was afflicted I went astray, but now I keep Your word" (Ps. 119:67).

"It is good for me that I have been afflicted, that I might learn Your statutes" (Ps. 119:71).

"Now if we are afflicted, it is for your consolation and salvation, which is effective for enduring the same sufferings which we also suffer. Or if we are comforted, it is for your consolation and salvation. And our hope for you is steadfast, because we know that as you are partakers of the sufferings, so also you will partake of the consolation" (2 Cor. 1:6, 7).

> **If you are experiencing trials, sufferings, or afflictions, God has a plan for your life.**

I was satisfied with the scriptures and the specificity of their answers. God had a purpose in allowing trials and afflictions in my life. Through these trials, He got my undivided attention. He had a message for me to bear. He wanted me to tell other hurting, grieving, and discouraged mothers and relatives that their struggles and trials will end.

Ellen White explains:

> If the Lord desires us to bear a message to Nineveh, it will not be as pleasing to Him for us to go to Joppa or to Capernaum. He has reasons for sending us to the place toward which our feet have been directed. At that very place there may be someone in need of the help we can give. He who sent Philip to the Ethiopian councilor, Peter to the Roman centurion, and the little Israelitish maiden to the help of Naaman, the Syrian captain, sends men and women and youth today as His representatives to those in need of divine help and guidance. (*The Ministry of Healing*, p. 473)

If you are experiencing trials, sufferings, or afflictions, God has a plan for your life. Ask Him, and He will give you the answer.

CHAPTER 3

Here Am I, Send Me

Also I heard the voice of the Lord, saying:
"Whom shall I send, and who will go for Us?"
Then I said, "Here am I! Send me."
—Isaiah 6:8

I was completely devastated when my only child was expelled from the university. She returned home to live with me. Instantly, my home became a war zone as Satan declared my home His territory. He directed all the weapons of His arsenal at us. The war was intense! The Bible records, in Revelation 12:7–9: "And war broke out in heaven: Michael and his angels fought with the dragon; and the dragon and his angels fought, but they did not prevail, nor was a place found for them in heaven any longer. So the great dragon was cast out, that serpent of old, called the Devil and Satan, who deceives the whole world; he was cast to the earth, and his angels were cast out with him."

Lucifer was the enemy that was cast to this earth and that entered my home. Revelation 12:10 says, "for the accuser of our brethren, who accused them before our God day and night, has been cast down." How could I cast him out of my home when he seemed so powerful? I realized that the enemy was very real and relentless. Wanting to destroy my family, he would stop at nothing to achieve his goal. However, there was One who is more powerful and readily available to fight for us. The Bible gave me scriptural confirmation when I prayed. *Michael* would fight the battle for me and win. "The LORD will fight for you, and you shall hold your peace" (Exod. 14:14). "For the LORD your God is He who goes with you, to fight for you against your enemies, to save you" (Deut. 20:14).

The effect of the war was evident in the violence that the enemy unleashed in our lives. There was hatred, a broken mother-daughter relationship, devastated emotions, crushed dreams, anger, deceit, verbal abuse, lying, and betrayal. There was a real spiritual war between Christ and Satan. It enveloped my home and attacked my daughter and me like an unrelenting monster storm ready to destroy anyone in its path. In this raging, unrelenting storm, we lashed out at and pelted each other with words that would have destroyed our relationship had Jesus not intervened. We were pawns in a real life battle that had eternal and deadly consequences. Our salvation was at stake. But the word of the Lord is: "So then my beloved, brethren, let every man be swift to hear, slow to speak for the wrath of man does not produce the righteousness of God" (James 1:19, 20).

I was unprepared for Satan's assaults, which were furious and vicious. Both my daughter and I were badly wounded. Most of the wounds were life threatening, and I thought the battle was lost. However, God stepped in and brought the roar of the battle to a standstill. God bound our wounds, preventing us from bleeding to a slow, untimely death in which we would both lose our salvation. He assured me with this promise: "He heals the brokenhearted and binds up their wounds" (Ps. 147:3).

As I experienced this crisis, the Holy Spirit instructed me to consider the following counsel from God's Word: "Be sober, be vigilant; because your adversary the devil walks about like a roaring lion, seeking whom he may devour" (1 Peter 5:8). He also had me remember the words of Paul, "My grace is sufficient for you, for My strength is made perfect in weakness" (2 Cor. 12:9).

Satan, the adversary, accuser, and devourer of souls, wanted to destroy our lives. He is God's arch-adversary and the sworn enemy of human beings. Because I am a child of God, because I am becoming more and more like Jesus, Satan hates me. His strategy has been to destroy and defeat my child and prevent us from experiencing a relationship with our Creator and Redeemer.

To defeat his strategy, the Holy Spirit inspired me to be sober and vigilant and to keep a clear mind with a definite plan for the attacks of Satan.

"Start an intentional, laser-focused prayer life," He told me.

I immediately began developing a radical prayer life, interceding fervently for myself and my child and patterning my prayer life after one aspect of Jesus' prayer life. "Now in the morning, having risen a long while before daylight, He went out and departed to a solitary place; and there He prayed" (Mark 1:35).

Note Ellen White's comment on Jesus' prayer life:

> Not for Himself, but for others, He lived and thought and prayed. From hours spent with God He came forth morning by morning, to bring the light of heaven to men. Daily He received a fresh baptism of the Holy Spirit. In the early hours of the new day the Lord awakened Him from His slumbers, and His soul and His lips were anointed with grace, that He might impart to others. (*Christ's Object Lessons*, p. 139)

Though developing such a radical prayer life, I yearned to have a closer experience with God as Jesus had with Him. I desired a more intimate relationship with the Lord.

"How would I develop this experience?" I pondered. "Holy Spirit, will You guide me through this experience?" I asked.

He did.

The Holy Spirit awakened me early one morning to commune with Him, with the Father, and with Jesus. I interceded earnestly and passionately for strength to bear my trials and for the Holy Spirit to give me clear and precise directions for my life.

"Show me Your ways, O LORD; teach me Your paths. Lead me in Your truth and teach me, for You are the God of my salvation; on You I wait all the day" (Ps. 25:4, 5).

I presented my case to the Lord and pleaded with Him to continue to answer my prayers from the Scriptures. This would be the sign that the Holy Spirit was with me.

As I interceded, the Holy Spirit answered my prayer with Isaiah, chapter 6, where the young prophet was in vision and encountered the Lord personally for the first time. Prior to chapter 6, Isaiah was judgmental, caustic, and bitter towards his people. However, after he "saw the Lord sitting on a throne," in chapter 6, he was a transformed person, ready to serve God more effectively.

I saw that my life paralleled Isaiah's. Before I met the Lord, I was judgmental, caustic, and bitter. I did not know how to deal with my daughter or the crisis that we were embroiled in. Although I was not called to be a prophet, there are similarities in how Isaiah the prophet and I treated God's children.

The prophet Isaiah explained: "In the year that King Uzziah died, I saw the Lord sitting on a throne, high and lifted up, and the train of His robe filled the temple.... And one cried to another and said: 'Holy, holy, holy is the LORD of hosts; the whole earth is full of His glory'" (Isa. 6:1–3).

Uzziah reigned for fifty-two long years. Overall, he was a good king. However, his life ended tragically. The period of his death was a time of peril and crisis for Israel.

The year he died the Lord called the young Isaiah and confirmed him to be His prophet. The Lord gave him a message of reproof for Israel. That year he had a vision in which he saw the Holy One high and lifted up upon His throne.

He saw the manifestation of the glory of the Lord. The Lord exposed Isaiah to His glory so He would look above the crisis around him. He saw the Lord seated upon His throne in heaven. "This manifestation of the divine glory took place upon the occasion of one of Isaiah's visits to the sacred precincts of the Temple (*Prophets and Kings*, p. 307). God designed that Isaiah should catch a wider vision than merely what he saw taking place about him. God would have him know that in spite of all the might of Assyria, He was still supreme upon His throne and in control of the affairs of earth" (*The Seventh-day Adventist Bible Commentary*, vol. 4, pp. 127, 128).

Like Isaiah, who saw and encountered the Lord the year of the tragedy of king Uzziah's death, I was privileged to see and meet the Lord for the first time in my Christian journey the tragic year that my brilliant eighteen-year-old daughter was expelled from the university. This was a time of peril and crisis in our lives. The burden was heavy, and the assaults from Satan were relentless. Nevertheless, the Lord wanted me to know that He was still on the throne and in control of our lives. He wanted me to personalize this vision and make it very real and applicable for others to help them in their distress and times of crisis.

To better understand the significance and meaning of this vision and its application to my life, I read Ellen White's commentary on it. She wrote that Isaiah—

> ... stood under the portico of the temple. Suddenly the gate and the inner veil of the temple seemed to be uplifted or withdrawn, and he was permitted to gaze within, upon the holy of

holies, where even the prophet's feet might not enter. There rose up before him a vision of Jehovah sitting upon a throne high and lifted up, while the train of His glory filled the temple. On each side of the throne hovered the seraphim, their faces veiled in adoration, as they ministered before their Maker and united in the solemn invocation, "Holy, holy, holy, is the Lord of hosts: the whole earth is full of His glory," until post and pillar and cedar gate seemed shaken with the sound, and the house was filled with their tribute of praise. Isaiah 6:3.

As Isaiah beheld this revelation of the glory and majesty of his Lord, he was overwhelmed with a sense of the purity and holiness of God. How sharp the contrast between the matchless perfection of his Creator, and the sinful course of those who, with himself, had long been numbered among the chosen people of Israel and Judah! "Woe is me!" he cried; "for I am undone; because I am a man of unclean lips, and I dwell in the midst of a people of unclean lips: for mine eyes have seen the King, the Lord of hosts." Verse 5. Standing, as it were, in the full light of the divine presence within the inner sanctuary, he realized that if left to his own imperfection and inefficiency, he would be utterly unable to accomplish the mission to which he had been called. But a seraph was sent to relieve him of his distress and to fit him for his great mission. A living coal from the altar was laid upon his lips, with the words, "Lo, this hath touched thy lips; and thine iniquity is taken away, and thy sin purged." [Isa. 6:7.] (*Prophets and Kings*, p. 307).

It was then that I heard the voice of the Lord saying, "Whom shall I send, and who will go for Us?" (Isa. 6:8).

And then I responded, "Here I am! send me."

The angel instructed Isaiah to go warn the people about God's approaching judgment if they chose not to change their evil ways.

As I read the vision, I meditated upon and internalized it, visualizing myself standing where Isaiah stood. When I did, I was overwhelmed with the purity and holiness of the holy God. This vision was designed to help me catch a clearer glimpse of my ungodliness and unrighteousness. It was also designed to help me gain a broader vision of what was taking place in my daughter's life and mine. Unbeknownst to me, God had a great plan for my life.

> As I read the vision, I meditated upon and internalized it, visualizing myself standing where Isaiah stood.

God wanted to let me know that, despite all the challenges that my daughter was experiencing, He was still on the throne and still maintained control of our lives. "For I know the thoughts that I think toward you, says the LORD, thoughts of peace and not of evil, to give you a future and a hope. Then you will call upon Me and go and pray to Me, and I will listen to you. And you will seek Me and find Me, when you search for Me with all your heart" (Jer. 29:11–13). I did not know that the Lord had such an extraordinary plan for my life. As with Joseph, He used a situation, which Satan meant for evil, to effect positive changes in our lives.

"Woe is me!" I cried, "for I am a woman of unclean lips, and I live with unclean people."

I continued at the portico and gazed into the sinless face of my Redeemer, the Holy One. I desired to have the Holy Spirit work with me to warn my child about the impending judgment that would come to us if we did not change our ways and listen to the Lord.

I continued reading the vision. Isaiah was overwhelmed and distressed that he was not good enough to accomplish the mission of a prophet. God saw his perplexity. He dispatched one of the heavenly seraphim from His glory to minister to Isaiah. The seraphim touched Isaiah's lips with a live coal taken from the altar and said, "Lo, this hath touched thine lips;

and thine iniquity is taken away, and thy sin purged" (Isa. 6:7, KJV). That was the same altar of intercession identified in Exodus 30:1–10.

John also had a similar experience on the Isle of Patmos when he wrote, "Then another angel, having a golden censer, came and stood at the altar. He was given much incense, that he should offer it with the prayers of all the saints upon the golden altar which was before the throne. And the smoke of the incense, with the prayers of the saints, ascended before God from the angel's hands" (Rev. 8:3, 4).

I was humbled and broken. In the presence of the holy God, I saw my own sinfulness and was more conscious of my own faults and corruptness. The vision taught me that, when God shows people His glory, they must be transformed and turn away from their sinful ways.

Once again I cried: "Woe is me! for I am a woman of unclean lips, and I live with unclean people."

I gazed into His sinless face and yearned to be more like the Holy One. I desired to have the Holy Spirit work with me so that I could feed my child and her friends with the same nourishing food of life. I agree with Ellen White when she wrote: "The Holy Spirit will come to all who are begging for the bread of life to give to their neighbors" (*Testimonies for the Church*, vol. 6, p. 90).

I stared at the altar of incense, which represented the work of Jesus as He presents before His Father the prayers of His people mixed with His righteousness. I meditated on the importance of prayer. As I saw the incense rising in the sanctuary, I saw my prayers—especially those for my daughter—rising to the heavenly throne of God. I lingered at the altar of incense for a very long time.

I recognized that my prayer life was powerless and oh so feeble! I needed much bolder and more fervent seasons of prayer. *How was I connecting with God when I prayed?* I meditated upon the importance and power of prayer. *How much time was I spending in prayer?*

"In keeping me at the altar of incense so long, was the Lord calling me to the ministry of intercession?"

"Yes," was the Holy Spirit's answer.

Then He assured me with this beautiful promise: "Oh, taste and see that the LORD is good ... Depart from evil and do good; seek peace and pursue it" (Psalm 34:8, 14).

That morning He cleansed my lips with a live coal taken from the altar. He had chosen me for a special work. It was a work of prayer. I was to pray for my salvation and my daughter's salvation and the salvation of the children of this world. He wants to save us.

Then He assured me with this beautiful promise, "Delight yourself also in the LORD, and He shall give you the desires of your heart" (Ps. 37:4). That morning He cleansed my lips with the live coal because He wanted His desires to be mine. Paul echoed that divine truth, when he wrote: "Brethren, my heart's desire and prayer to God for Israel is that they may be saved" (Rom. 10:1). It is the Lord's yearning that all His children be saved, and that includes my child!

Much like Isaiah, I was petrified that the Lord was calling me for service. Before I could intercede for others, the Lord had to purify me. A live coal touched my lips, and He cleansed my iniquity and my sins. That morning I was transformed at the altar of incense. The cleansing of my lips was the Lord's confirmation that He had called me to a very sacred and privileged ministry of mediating for others. Like Isaiah, I also heard the voice of the Lord, saying, "Whom shall I send to go for Us, to intercede for the children who have left the church? Who will intercede for those who are in the church and need to have a closer relationship with Me? Whom shall I send to encourage parents—especially single mothers—whose children have left the church and are being severely attacked by Satan? Who will stand in the gap and pray for these My beloved children? Who will go to the war zone and pray for My lost children?"

Then I said, "Here I am, Lord, send me."

The first "Intercessory Prayer Ministry Praying Moms International" started immediately after this encounter. A prayer ministry for my local church soon followed.

CHAPTER 4

Live! Live! Live!

*And when I passed by you and saw you struggling
in your own blood, I said to you in your blood, "Live!"
Yes, I said to you in your blood, "Live!"*
—Ezekiel 16:6

When the Lord is about to do a great, exciting work in your life, Satan moves upon someone to object or interfere. This chapter will illustrate the ongoing drama between good and evil between God and Satan. Satan attempted to use the actions of a surgeon to prevent God from fulfilling His plan for my life. God had entrusted a prayer ministry to me, and Satan was livid with rage. He hated me, and he attempted to prevent me from getting God's blessing in God's call for me to start a prayer ministry to teach others how to develop an intimate relationship with God through prayer.

How did he do this? He tried to kill me. And how did he try to kill me? You are about to find out.

This chapter reveals the mighty power of God to overrule Satan's plans. A miracle happened when He intervened and saved my life. I was destined to die alone that night as I struggled in a pool of my own blood. However, God demonstrated His mercy in healing me when I was not ready to die. I claimed the promise: "Heal me, O LORD, and I shall be healed; save me, and I shall be saved, for You are my praise" (Jer. 17:14).

How can I die and leave my teenage daughter alone? I thought.

Jesus had the answer. As I lay dying in a pool of my own blood, He consulted immediately with the angels.

"Go rescue my child!" He ordered them.

Like a flash of lightning, the angels left heaven. They alighted in my room and said, "And when I passed by you and saw you struggling in your own blood, I said to you in your blood, 'Live!'" (Ezek. 16:6).

Ellen White describes the ministry of the angels:

> In all ages, angels have been near to Christ's faithful followers. The vast confederacy of evil is arrayed against all who would overcome; but Christ would have us look to the things which are not seen, to the armies of heaven encamped about all who love God, to deliver them. From what dangers, seen and unseen, we have been preserved through the interposition of the angels, we shall never know, until in the light of eternity we see the providences of God. Then we shall know that the whole family of heaven was interested in the family here below, and that messengers from the throne of God attended our steps from day to day. (*The Desire of Ages*, p. 240)

Why was I lying alone, struggling in my own blood ready to die? Two days prior, I had a simple colonoscopy procedure, which was completed without any complications. After twenty-four hours, I returned to work. It was an uneventful day. I experienced no discomfort or bleeding. I was excited that the doctor had satisfactorily removed a benign polyp.

On the prayer line that night, we thanked God for His goodness to me. Like the psalmist, I echoed: "Oh, give thanks to the LORD! Call upon His name; make known His deeds among the peoples! Sing to Him, sing psalms to Him; Talk of all His wondrous works!" (Ps. 105:1, 2). We prayed, and all were agreed in the power of united prayer. We prayed that God's will be done in our lives. Jesus promised: "Again I say to you that if two of you agree on earth concerning anything that they ask, it will be done for them by My Father in heaven. For where two or three are gathered together in My name, I am there in the midst of them" (Matt. 18:19, 20).

Ellen White commented on the necessity of united prayer. "Those who meet together for prayer will receive an unction from the Holy One. There is great need of secret prayer, but there is also need that several Christians meet together and unite with earnestness their petitions to God" (*In Heavenly Places*, p. 91).

We spent almost two hours on the prayer line, thanking God, praising Him, and rejoicing in His mercy, healing, and goodness "The melody of praise is the atmosphere of heaven; and when heaven comes in touch with the earth, there is music and song—'thanksgiving and the voice of melody' Isaiah 51:3" (*Education*, p. 161).

Immediately after finishing our session with the prayer line, I felt an urgent need to urinate. I rushed to the bathroom. To my shock, I heard a gushing sound! The bowl was almost full of blood! I staggered to my room. Lying down on the bed, I felt dazed and disoriented. Instantly there was another feeling of urgency. Again I heard another gush like a broken pipe. I wobbled to my room. This time I did not reach the bed. I fell with a loud thud on the floor and lay in a pool of my own blood, grasping for my very life. Alone and unready to die. I faded in and out of consciousness. I do not know how long I was in that condition, but it seemed that I was destined to die in my own blood that very night.

Satan thought he could kill me to keep me from fulfilling God's calling to lead out in prayer ministry. It was that ministry that had changed my life. Satan observed the change as I developed a more intimate relationship with God. Satan knew that God was about to accomplish something great in my life, and he wanted to prevent that from happening. However, God would not let him succeed. The grip of power he had held over me for over twenty years had been broken.

Twenty years prior, I left the church and my faith after graduating as an elementary school teacher. I relocated to the United States and forgot the One who brought me here. The glimmer and glitter of the big city, of money, and of my education all clouded my mind. My mother and family prayed for my salvation. However, my mother died before I returned to Christ and His true church. I am eagerly awaiting our meeting at the first resurrection when Jesus returns.

I came back to church after spending many years on Satan's ground. I also began returning a faithful tithe and offerings and held several offices in the church. Nevertheless, I was still not a Christian, a real follower of Jesus. Satan was very angry that he had lost one of his followers.

Angels that excel in strength were dispatched to my side. Hebrews, chapter 1, describes the role of the angels: "Are they not all ministering spirits sent forth to minister for them who will inherit salvation?" (Heb. 1:14).

Ellen White describes these powerful heavenly agents:

> Could men see with heavenly vision, they would behold companies of angels that excel in strength stationed about those who have kept the word of Christ's patience. With sympathizing tenderness, angels have witnessed their distress and have heard their prayers. They are waiting the word of their Commander to snatch them from their peril. (*The Great Controversy*, p. 630)

That night powerful angels were speedily dispatched to my house to save me from death.

It was a miracle of grace that, while I got weaker and weaker lying in my blood, I did not die. The marvel is that an angel passed by and saw me and shouted, "Live! Live! Live!"

As I lay on the floor, it seemed that someone held my hand and gently picked me up, leading me around the bed to the telephone. I was very dizzy and lightheaded. I tried to dial 911. It was busy! I dialed 911 again. It was still busy! I was so lightheaded that I could not see the keypad on the telephone. Satan was determined to kill me that night by keeping me from dialing 911.

"Live! Live!" shouted the angel. I dialed 911 once more. An operator answered. I described my situation in a rambling, confused voice.

"Are you alone?" she asked.

"Yes," I replied, fading in and out of consciousness.

"Can you open the door?"

"I will try."

The angel held my hand and led me to the door. I was weak, pale, and ready to collapse again. I opened the door. Within minutes the ambulance arrived.

Miraculously, I regained consciousness. I called my niece, Marcia, who was on the prayer line with me. She was instrumental in my return to the true church. One night on the prayer line she informed me that, after I left the church, she was very concerned about my salvation. While she was a teen, the possibility that I would lose my salvation weighed heavily on her mind. She prayed sincerely and passionately for me. She felt that she needed an army of prayer warriors to pray with her for my salvation. She sent my name in to the Voice of Prophecy, requesting prayer for me. The power of intercessory prayer was made on my behalf. I was rescued, and Satan was angry because my niece dared to pray for me. It was the LORD who called me to intercessory prayer ministry.

My niece and my daughter arrived minutes before the ambulance left. They were shocked to see my condition. I was pale, wan, and almost lifeless. They were even more startled when they saw the blood-soaked off-white carpet. It was in the providence of God that they both arrived at the same time.

The Holy Spirit knew that my daughter, then a teenager, would need support in this stressful time. Thus, He prepared someone to console her. As I was driven away in the ambulance, she called out: "Don't die, Mommy! Don't die, Mommy!" My niece and daughter followed in their car. Months after the incident my daughter told me that she knew something terrible had happened to me that night. Peter is right when he is recorded saying in Acts 2:39 that the promise of the Holy Spirit is for us and our children who are "afar off." The Holy Spirit prepared my daughter for the crisis she was about to confront.

> **As I was driven away in the ambulance, she called out: "Don't die, Mommy! Don't die, Mommy!"**

I was rushed to the nearest hospital. After some hours in the emergency department, they transferred me to a regular ward. The bleeding stabilized for a short time. However, within a few hours, I was hurriedly moved into the intensive care unit where I spend two days.

What was the cause of the profuse bleeding? A day after the colonoscopy I had developed a "catastrophic internal hemorrhage called exsanguination (also known colloquially as "bleeding out," "a drain of blood," or "to make bloodless"), the fatal process of hypovolemia (blood loss) to the degree sufficient to cause death." The surgeon failed to cauterize the incision site (that is, to fuse the tissues by application of heat) after removing the benign polyp. This was the reason for the severe bleeding.

If the Holy Spirit had not prompted me to go to the bathroom, I would have fallen asleep. The blood would have pooled in my abdominal cavity. I would have died in my sleep from hypovolemia.

As the nurse administered several units of blood I reminded her that Jesus' blood was shed to save my life and "Jesus' blood can save your life, too," I told her.

She smiled in agreement and continued infusing the blood to save my life.

The following day, another colonoscopy was performed. This time, the surgeon cauterized the site. After a day I was discharged to go home, and I joyfully praised the Lord.

> Bless the LORD, O my soul; and all that is within me, bless His holy name! Bless the LORD, O my soul, and forget not all His benefits: who forgives all your iniquities, who heals all your diseases, who redeems your life from destruction, who crowns you with lovingkindness and tender mercies, who satisfies your mouth with good things, so that your youth is renewed like the eagle's. (Ps. 103:1–5)

This whole experience confirmed my belief that there is a real war going on between Christ and Satan, and my child and I were caught up in it. Had it not been for the mercies of God, you would not be reading this book. God overruled Satan's plan and I have been able to write my story so that the world could hear how God has carried out His plans for my life. I agree with Paul when he wrote that it is "not by works of righteousness which we have done, but according to His mercy He saved us, through the washing of regeneration and renewing of the Holy Spirit" (Titus 3:5).

CHAPTER 5

Praying Moms International

*I have heard your prayer, I have seen
your tears; ... I will deliver you.*
—Isaiah 38:5, 6

Praying Moms International is a powerful Christ-centered intercessory prayer ministry, ordained and designed by the Lord. I accepted the challenge to be an intercessor after I had a most convicting and convincing encounter with God. He used the vision documented in Isaiah 6 to start this ministry. This ministry teaches heartbroken mothers and relatives how to become powerful intercessors for their children who live in the war zone of planet Earth.

In this world, a great conflict is raging for the souls of our children. It is a war between God and Satan that started in heaven and has continued on earth after the cherubim Lucifer, who sat next to God, was kicked out of heaven. He brought the war to the human family as he engaged Eve in a conversation in the Garden of Eden, questioning God's motives.

When Eve doubted God's goodness, she fell into Satan's lying trap. She was deceived. Her husband Adam subsequently followed her in sin. This tragedy escalated the spiritual war on earth. In this war, there can be no neutrals, no noncombatants. As mothers and concerned relatives, we have a choice. We are either on God's side or on Satan's. In our ministry, we choose to be on God's side because the salvation of our children is under severe attack. Spiritual missiles, bombs, mortars, and hand grenades are hurled at them daily. They are unprepared to fight this war for themselves. Therefore, we volunteer to be prayer warriors on their behalf.

The mission of this ministry is to:

1. Mediate and ask the Holy Spirit to reclaim all of God's lost and missing children
2. Intercede on behalf of our children who are in the church that they remain faithful and true to the Lord.

"Praying Moms International" has claimed, as its text of inspiration, God's promise, "I have heard your prayer, I have seen your tears; ... I will deliver you" (Isa. 38:5, 6).

Why this text? One night as I was facedown on the floor crying my heart out, I pleaded with the Lord to protect my daughter from the dangers and perils of the night. I cried out and asked Him to give me a scripture to confirm that He heard my prayer and that He would answer it. Immediately, there was a very strong impression. "Get up and read Isaiah 38." So I did. My heart swelled with joy as I read, "I have heard your prayer, I have seen your tears; ... I will deliver you" (Isa. 38:5, 6). I read the chapter over and over until I grasped the importance and power of prayer. Isaiah 38 describes King Hezekiah of Judah who was sick unto death. He received a message from God through the prophet Isaiah, "'Thus says the LORD: "Set your house in order, for you shall die and not live."' Then Hezekiah turned his face toward the wall, and prayed to the LORD, and said,

'Remember now, O LORD, I pray, how I have walked with before You in truth and with a loyal heart, and have done what is good in Your sight.'"

God answered King Hezekiah, "Thus says the Lord, the God of David your father, 'I have heard your prayers, I have seen your tears; … I will deliver you …'" (Isa. 38:2–6). If God answered Hezekiah's prayer certainly He will answer our prayers about our children about whom the psalmist declared, "Children are a heritage from the LORD, the fruit from the womb is a reward" (Ps. 127:3). If we do not passionately intercede for our children, they will die.

"Yes, there is a God who cares and answers prayers specifically," I cried.

The power of God to answer prayers became real to me. This answer started me on a journey of asking the Lord to answer all my prayers with scripture. I was overwhelmed as He continued to fulfill my request. I have received thousands of answers from scripture, and I continue to receive scriptural answers. My faith in God has increased as He continues to honor my request.

> The power of God to answer prayers became real to me.

Many mothers have used this model and received tremendous blessings from the scriptural answers. The Bible says: "All Scripture is given by inspiration of God, and is profitable for doctrine, for reproof, for correction, for instruction in righteousness, that the man of God may be complete, thoroughly equipped for every good work" (2 Tim. 3:16, 17).

The Holy Spirit revealed God's will for my life through the Scriptures. He showed me how to live a life that is pleasing to Him and that would influence my daughter and all I meet. This contact and positive interaction with Jesus through the Scriptures was the foundation I needed to lead my daughter and other children back to the Lord.

Note Ellen White's comments about the role of the Holy Scriptures.

> The Holy Scriptures are the perfect standard of truth, and as such should be given the highest place in education. To obtain an education worthy of the name, we must receive a knowledge of God, the Creator, and of Christ, the Redeemer, as they are revealed in the sacred word. Every human being, created in the image of God, is endowed with a power akin to that of the Creator—individuality, power to think and to do.... As the perfection of His character is dwelt upon, the mind is renewed, and the soul is re-created in the image of God... Higher than the highest human thought can reach is God's ideal for His children. Godliness—godlikeness—is the goal to be reached. (*Education*, pp. 17, 18)

That is how we intercede on behalf of our children.

What joy will be ours when we get to heaven and the Lord welcomes all the children we have prayed for. What a thrill it will be when Jesus declares, "Here am I and the children whom the LORD has given me!" (Isa. 8:18), and when the parents of those children respond in excitement, "These are the ones who come out of the great tribulation, and washed their robes and made them white in the blood of the Lamb" (Rev. 7:14).

Jesus lovingly assures mothers and other relatives, "Because you contended with Me and prayed without ceasing, enter the joy of My kingdom." As the crown of God's acceptance is graciously placed on the head of each child and their parents, the redeemed will declare: "Amen! Blessing and glory and wisdom; thanksgiving and honor and power and might, be to our God forever and ever. Amen" (Rev. 7:12).

This beautiful picture will be realized when there is a "Praying Moms International" ministry in every local congregation around the world.

At the Power of Prayer meetings, connected with this ministry, mothers, grandmothers, cousins, aunts, friends, and other female relatives meet together weekly for an hour of power praying for children. Attendees are committed to presenting to the Lord in prayer the needs of the children of the church, the community, and the world.

In these meetings, we lift our hands heavenward. We cry out to the Lord for the lives of our children who do not know that they are lost nor even care about their salvation. The world that they live in encourages self-determination and a life without God. Many of them are not spiritually strong or grounded in the Lord, and they have accepted Satan's lie. Therefore we, as mothers, are commanded by the Holy Spirit to intercede passionately for them.

Unbelievable changes have occurred in the lives of the intercessors and in the lives of the children for whom we have prayed. Backsliders have been reconverted, grades have improved, disobedient children have become respectful, school fees have been paid, and children have been accepted into prestigious universities and colleges. God has taken control of the lives of our loved ones because we have dared to pray passionately and fervently for them.

> **Unbelievable changes have occurred in the lives of the intercessors and in the lives of the children for whom we have prayed.**

Preparing for an Intercessory Prayer Ministry

Following are the steps required to establish an intercessory prayer ministry:

1. Begin a passionate radical intentional prayer life. "Pray without ceasing" (1 Thess. 5:17).
2. Ask the Holy Spirit to teach you how to pray, as the disciples asked Jesus: "Lord, teach us to pray" (Luke 11:1). Just as Jesus taught His disciples how to pray, so the Holy Spirit will teach you when you ask.

3. Confess your sins to the Lord. "If we confess our sins, He is faithful and just to forgive our sins" (1 John 1:9).
4. Like Solomon, pray for wisdom that you can be a great leader. "And God gave Solomon wisdom and exceedingly great understanding ..." (1 Kings 4:29).
5. Pray for an understanding heart to discern between good and evil. "Therefore give to Your servant an understanding heart ... that I may discern between good and evil...." (1 Kings 3:9).
6. Encourage mothers, aunts, cousins, grandmothers, and any other biological or spiritual relative to participate. Pray with and for each other. "Pray for one another" (James 5:16).

How to Start a Prayer Group

Following are the things you need to do to form a prayer group.

1. Start with one or as many mothers, parents, or relatives committed to crying to the Lord for their children in a weekly "Hour of Power" prayer meeting.
2. Bring the following items:
    a. A Bible
    b. A songbook
    c. A Spirit of Prophecy book
    d. Other books on prayer.
3. Use the following format:
    a. The leader should bring a verse of scripture or a passage from the Spirit of Prophecy that she has selected about the power of intercessory prayer.
    b. The meeting should cover praise, thanksgiving, confession, intercession, praise, and the claiming of God's promises for our children. The meeting should begin and end with praise. An assigned member of the group should read the scripture.

The Power of Intercession

The format of the meeting adds to its power:

1. Make your prayer request known to the group, that is, the "prayer points."
2. Spend an hour interceding on behalf of the children.
3. End by singing a prayer song.
4. Hug each other after praying.
5. Plan to return the next week bringing a new member.
6. Remember that God hears; God cares; God answers.

Prayer Points

The leader of the group guides the group's members in praying for specific "prayer points." "Prayer points" are specific outcomes that challenge the people of God to be persistent and steadfast in prayer until God intervenes. This was the method that was so effective in our meetings.

There are many examples of "prayer points" in the Bible. Here are a few:

In Ephesians 6:18, 19, Paul states, "Praying always ... that utterance may be given to me, that I may open my mouth boldly to make known the mystery of the gospel." His prayer point was specific.

Nehemiah was also very specific. "O Lord, I pray, please let Your ear be attentive to the prayer of Your servant, and to the prayer of Your servants who desire to fear Your name; and let Your servant prosper this day, I pray, and grant him mercy in the sight of this man" (Neh. 1:11).

Hannah prayed: "O LORD of hosts, if You will indeed look on the affliction of Your maidservant and remember me, and not forget Your maidservant, but will give Your maidservant a male child, then I will give him to the LORD all the days of his life, and no razor shall come upon his head" (1 Sam. 1:11).

It is important to observe that all intercessors in the Bible were always specific in their prayer requests.

The desired outcomes are expressed as simple prayers in brief sentences. These sentences do not prevent spontaneity in prayer but are intended to give focus to the mother's intercessory prayer.

A "prayer point" has the following makeup:

1. Expression of need
2. A desired outcome
3. Intercessory prayer
4. Divine intervention.

There are different types of prayer points, which include:

1. Global prayer points
2. National prayer points
3. Personal prayer points
4. Evangelistic prayer points.

An effective group prayer leader cultivates the habit of writing out prayer points. Written prayer points give focus to the prayer. Following are different types of prayer points:

1. Confession of sins
2. Confession of your child's sins
3. Asking forgiveness for sins that you have committed that may have affected your child's life, such as being mean to him or her.
4. Requests for reconciliation between parent and child.

These should be prayed daily.

**"Prayer Points," the prayer points definition, makeup, and different types used by permission from Pastor Telemaques' book *The Power of Prayer in Evangelism*.

Praying God's Word over Your Children

The highlight of the "Hour of Power Prayer Meeting" was praying God's Word back to Him. We claimed His promises as we interceded passionately for our children.

These are some of the promises the Lord gave me as I prayed relentlessly for my daughter. I shared these promises with our group. We pleaded with the Lord to fulfill His promises in our children's lives.

- We thank You, Lord, that You promised us in Isaiah 43:5, 6: "Fear not, for I am with you; I will bring your descendants from the east, and gather you from the west; I will say to the north, 'Give them up!' and to the south, 'Do not keep them back!' Bring My sons from afar, and My daughters from the ends of the earth."
- We thank You, Lord, that You promised to pour out the Holy Spirit in our children's lives. We claim the promise recorded in Acts 2:38, 39: "Repent, and let every one of you be baptized in the name of Jesus Christ for the remission of sins; and you shall receive the gift of the Holy Spirit. For the promise is to you and your children, and to all who afar off, as many as the Lord our God will call."
- We thank You, Lord, that You promised us that we should stop weeping because there is hope in the future for us and our children. "Refrain your voice from weeping, and your eyes from tears; for your work shall be rewarded, says the Lord, and they shall come back from the land of the enemy. There is hope in the future, says the LORD, that your children shall come back to their own border" (Jer. 31:16, 17).
- We thank You, Lord, that You have heard our prayers on behalf of our children's salvation. Thank You for Your promise to save them in Isaiah: "For I will contend with him who contends with you, and I will save your children" (Isa. 49:25).
- We thank You, Lord, for giving us the confidence to believe that, if we ask anything according to Your will, You will hear us. We know that it is your will that they be saved. Peter wrote in his second epistle:

"The Lord is not slack concerning His promise, as some count slackness, but is longsuffering toward us, not willing that any should perish but that all should come to repentance" (2 Peter 3:9). John wrote in his first epistle, "Now this is the confidence that we have in Him, that if we ask anything according to His will, He hears us. And if we know that He hears us, whatever we ask, we know that we have the petitions that we have asked of Him" (1 John 5:14, 15). "

- We cling to these promises and patiently wait for you to fulfil Your word in their lives through the hope of eternal life that is in your word of truth. Numbers 23:19 says: "God is not a man, that He should lie ..."
- We thank You, Lord, for Your promise recorded in Isaiah 54:17: "No weapon formed against you shall prosper, and every tongue which rises against you in judgment you will condemn."
- We thank You, Lord, for the mothers of the Bible who experienced challenges. They are our models and inspiration. They prayed, and You answered their prayers.
- We thank You for answering our prayers as well.

Three major examples of praying mothers in Scripture are:

1. Sarah (Genesis 18).
2. Hannah (1 Samuel 1, 2)
3. Elizabeth (Luke 1:41–45).

- We thank you for the devoted women who preceded us. They embodied the biblical foundation for our praying for our children. They inspire us to act as prayer warriors for our children. We recognize that there were other praying mothers, such as—

Susanna Wesley, who was the mother of Methodist reformers Charles and John Wesley, the latter himself becoming a great prayer warrior. Susanna was married to a preacher. However, her home life was hopeless. Instead of giving up on her husband and children, she prayed without ceasing. As a young woman, she had committed her life to the Lord. She promised Him that, for every hour she spent on entertainment, she would give the Lord an hour in prayer. However, this proved impossible to fulfill. There was no time for entertainment, so there was no time for prayer. She was overwhelmed in taking care of her husband and nineteen children, including one who was physically challenged and needed constant care, another who did not talk until he was six years old, and a daughter who got pregnant out of wedlock, and the man who got her pregnant did not marry her. In addition, she herself was a very sick woman.

How was a mother to cope with such life circumstances? She knew the answer—pray." She decided to pray for two hours daily. She knew that, if she did not pray, she would still have to give the Lord an account for her life and for the children she had received at His blessing.

The Holy Spirit moved upon her, and she devised a plan for daily prayer. She told her children that, when they saw her with her apron over her head, it meant that she was praying and must not be disturbed. The Lord intervened in her life. Two of her sons—John and Charles—became powerful preachers for the Lord and founded the Methodist Episcopal Church. Their ministries transformed the lives of millions of people. John once preached to a crowd of over 32,000 people without a microphone. His brother Charles became a prolific hymn writer, composing over nine thousand hymns. Many of these are sung in churches today. One of my favorite hymns is "Jesus Lover of My Soul." (Insights from the internet)

I too was impacted by a praying mother. Thank God for praying mothers! Another phenomenal praying mother I have admired and after whom I have patterned my prayer life is Monica, the mother of Augustine.

- We thank You, Lord, for her testimony.

We are told: "The mother of Augustine prayed for her son's conversion. She saw no evidence that the Spirit of God was impressing his heart, but she was not discouraged. She laid her finger upon the texts, presenting before God His own words, and pleaded as only a mother can. Her deep humiliation, her earnest importunities, her unwavering faith, prevailed, and the Lord gave her the desire of her heart..." (*Testimonies for the Church*, vol. 5, pp. 322, 323). Augustine had left home and followed the path that led him further and further away from Christ. He tried to outrun his mother's prayers but could not. He was convicted by the Holy Spirit, and his life was transformed. He confessed that his mother had wept for him many years, and, after she died, he was weeping for her.

These are two of the mothers who interceded passionately for their children. The outcome of their prayers they left in God's hands. And He heard and answered their prayers. Their children's lives were changed, and they came to influence millions. We can only imagine the outcome of these children's lives if their mothers had not prayed.

Our prophetess, Ellen White, was a woman of prayer and a great intercessor, and she was given practical counsel on how to pray for our children. She reminds us about the eternal consequences involved.

> You have brought children into the world who have had no voice in regard to their existence. You have made yourselves responsible in a great measure for their future happiness, their eternal well-being. The burden is upon you, whether you are sensible of it or not, to train these children for God, to watch with jealous care the first approach of the wily foe and be prepared to raise a standard against him. Build a fortification of prayer and faith about your children, and exercise diligent watching thereunto. You are not secure a moment against the attacks of Satan. You have no time to rest from watchful, earnest labor. You should not sleep a moment at your post. This is a most important warfare. Eternal consequences are involved. It is life or death with you and your family. Your only safety is to break your hearts before God and seek the kingdom of

heaven as little children. (*Testimonies for the Church*, vol. 2, pp. 397, 398)

Ellen White's inspired writings have been a tremendous blessing to our group. Ellen White wrote about raising godly children and the importance of prayer. If her counsels are consistently followed, it will prevent great heartache. She reminds us about the great rewards for daring to pray for our children. "With joy unutterable, parents see the crown, the robe, the harp, given to their children. The days of hope and fear are ended. The seed sown with tears and prayers may have seemed to be sown in vain, but their harvest is reaped with joy at last. Their children have been redeemed" (*Child Guidance*, p. 569).

"Praying Moms International" laid the foundation for prayer ministries in my local church and conference.

CHAPTER 6

A House of Prayer for All Nations

> Even them I will bring to My holy mountain, and make
> them joyful in My house of prayer. Their burnt offerings and
> their sacrifices will be accepted on My altar; for My house
> shall be called a house of prayer for all nations.
> —Isaiah 56:7

How does an ordinary member of a local congregation get the attention of the president of her conference to receive and act upon an extraordinary message from God?

I prayed earnestly and asked the Holy Spirit to go before me and convince the conference president that a message to start a prayer ministry in the conference was coming directly from God and not from the messenger.

When the Lord appointed His servant Cyrus to do a tremendous task, He promised him: "I will go before you and make the crooked places straight; …that you may know that I, the LORD, who call you by name, am the God of Israel" (Isa. 45:2, 3).

I pleaded with the Lord to go before me and soften the president's heart. The urgency of a prayer ministry in the conference was crucial to the fulfilling of the mission of the church. The Lord saw that revival and reformation is needed in the conference.

The Lord has called our Conference to intense prayer and supplication. After Solomon dedicated the temple, the Lord gave him a solemn warning and instruction, which is applicable to our conference today: "If My people who are called by My name and will humble themselves, and pray and seek My face, and turn from their wicked ways, then I will hear from heaven, and forgive their sin and heal their land. Now My eyes will be open and My ears attentive to prayer made in this place" (2 Chron. 7:14, 15). In my mind, this applied to the Southeastern Conference of Seventh-day Adventists.

So, what is the urgency in having a prayer ministry in the conference? Ellen White answers:

> A revival of true godliness among us is the greatest and most urgent of all our needs. To seek this should be our first work. There must be earnest effort to obtain the blessing of the Lord, not because God is not willing to bestow His blessing upon us, but because we are unprepared to receive it. Our heavenly Father is more willing to give His Holy Spirit to them that ask Him, than are earthly parents to give good gifts to their children. But it is our work, by confession, humiliation, repentance, and earnest prayer, to fulfill the conditions upon which God has promised to grant us His blessing. A revival need be expected only in answer to prayer. (*Selected Messages*, bk. 1, p. 121)

> **The urgency of a prayer ministry in the conference was crucial to the fulfilling of the mission of the church.**

Satan's greatest fear is that this promised revival will actually come. Revival always begins with one person being empowered by the Holy Spirit to do His work. Throughout history, the greatest revivals were the result of heartfelt intercession. The Lord has called the conference to experience a revival through united prayer. The apostle Paul reminds us, "Pray without ceasing" (1 Thess. 5:17). Note Ellen White's comments about united prayer.

> The Lord has promised that where two or three are met together in His name, there will He be in the midst. Those who meet together for prayer will receive an unction from the Holy One. There is great need of secret prayer, but there is also need that several Christians meet together and unite with earnestness their petitions to God. (*In Heavenly Places*, p. 91)

The apostolic church was consumed with prayer. Concerning the early church and the disciples, Luke records: "These all continued with one accord in prayer and supplication" (Acts 1:14). The Lord is calling our conference to intense prayer and supplication.

How was this to be accomplished? Who would God enlist to fulfill this mission?

"For the eyes of the LORD run to and fro to throughout the whole earth, to show Himself strong on behalf of those whose heart is loyal to Him" (2 Chron. 16:9). God wondered if there were a member in the conference that He could use as a channel for the outpouring of the Holy Spirit so that the conference could be a house of prayer for all nations. He looked at my life and character flaws and decided that I was the member that He would use as the instrument to fulfill this tremendous mission. However, I was very fearful that this task was too great for me.

He reminded me, "You did not choose Me, but I chose you and appointed you that you should go and bear fruit, and that your fruit should remain ..." (John 15:16). Nevertheless, I argued with the Holy Spirit.

"What shall I do?" I asked the Holy Spirit as I prayed earnestly.

"Send an email to President Willie Taylor. Tell Him to start a prayer ministry in the conference." This response was so impressive that it seemed almost audible.

Although the Lord had called me, I protested like a stubborn child.

"Why me, Lord?" I protested. "He does not know me. He might not respond. Ask someone he knows and trusts."

"Why not you?" was the response.

I could not answer. Immediately my mind reflected on the call of Moses to ministry when he argued and questioned God. He told the Lord, "'O my Lord, please send by the hand of whomever else You may send.' So the anger of the LORD was kindled against Moses" (Exod. 4:13, 14). Nevertheless, the kind and merciful God gave Moses the opportunity to complete the assignment that He had given him.

I did not want God's anger to be kindled against me. The Lord lovingly assured me that I was the person He wanted to use to convey the message to the president about starting a prayer ministry in the conference to start a revival and lead the members to a more powerful prayer life. This would require the members' having an intimate relationship with the Lord. Revival begins with individual members, spreading like a flame throughout the conference.

The prayer ended. In response to the command from God, I sent an email to the president. It was a simple message: "Mr. President, the Lord wants you to start a prayer ministry in the conference."

I received an immediate response. "Yes, I will start a prayer ministry in the conference. I can assure you that the Holy Spirit is working through you."

I was thrilled with the response. The Holy Spirit is still what Jesus said He is—"The Spirit of truth, whom the world cannot receive, because it neither sees Him nor knows Him; but you know Him, for He dwells with you and will be in you" (John 14:17). "When He is come, He will reprove the world of sin, and of righteousness, and of judgment" (John 16:8, KJV).

The president was aware that the Holy Spirit would guide the conference into all truth.

The Holy Spirit used an ordinary but willing woman to relay a message to the president of the conference, a message that changed the conference into a praying conference. That first contact developed into a cyber relationship with the president. I finally met him at Women's Ministry Conference. He told me then that, after I sent him the email to start a prayer ministry, he received several other emails with the same request for a prayer ministry. "You were the first member to ask me to start a prayer ministry in the conference," he said. I continued to email him, telling him about some of the miracles of answered prayers that I had seen on 3ABN, the independent Seventh-day Adventist satellite network.

He told me, "Prayer ministry is a priority for the conference. There is nothing more important than that the conference members seek this revival together." A year after I sent the initial email, an official prayer ministry was formed. Our conference was one of the first conferences in the Southern Union to have an official prayer ministry.

The miracle and leading of the Holy Spirit continued. The president, under the guidance of the Holy Spirit, entrusted the coordination and the leadership of the prayer ministry to his faithful Women's Ministry leader, Sister Nicolle Brise.

Plans were made for the inaugural prayer convocation to be held at the conference office. Note Ellen White's comments about prayer convocations:

> There is nothing more needed in the work than the practical results of communion with God. We should hold convocations for prayer, asking the Lord to open the way for the truth to enter the strongholds where Satan has set up his throne, and dispel the shadow he has cast athwart the pathway of those whom he is seeking to deceive and destroy. We have the assurance, "The effectual fervent prayer of a righteous man availeth much." James 5:16. (*In Heavenly Places*, p. 93)

I interceded passionately with the Holy Spirit for the right choice of people to participate in the inaugural meeting. The pastor who officiated at the meeting was a divine appointment. I watched 3ABN and was energized with Ruthie Jacobsen's "When God's People Pray" and with many other programs about prayer.

One of my nieces, Carol, knew that the Holy Spirit was guiding me into all truth through prayer. She watched a program on 3ABN and commented to me about it.

"You must hear this pastor's testimony about prayer," she said.

I prayed that the program would be rebroadcast. It was! I was excited after watching the program presented by Pastor Samuel Telemaque, Director of Personal Ministries, Sabbath School Director, and Prayer Coordinator for the Caribbean Union Conference. Currently, he serves as Sabbath School director and Director of Mission for the Inter-American Division of Seventh-day Adventists.

This was a powerful report about the power of prayer, reformation, and evangelism. Pastor Telemaque stated that he had seen "hundreds of people come to Christ in baptism through the power of prayer, the Holy Spirit, and the preaching of the Word." He remarked that the same success of bringing thousands of people to Jesus in the Inter-American Division can be replicated in any part of the world. "With God, all things are possible," he concluded.

The host asked him, "Pastor, can you come over to Macedonia and help us?" The host did not know how prophetic that invitation would prove. Nor did I know that the Holy Spirit had already appointed me to be instrumental in assisting in this process. After I watched the program, I was very excited to learn how the Lord was working with Pastor Telemaque's ministry to change lives through the power of prayer.

I sent an email immediately to President Taylor. I told him about the phenomenal experience of prayer and the work of the Holy Spirit in the Inter-American Division. I gave him detailed information about the pastor and suggested that he invite the pastor to participate in the inaugural prayer convocation. The president emailed me back. He wrote that he met Pastor Telemaque at a leaders' meeting and had invited him to be the presenter for the inaugural prayer convocation. Sister Nicolle Brise had also met Pastor Telemaque and had invited him to participate.

"The Holy Spirit is working," was my response.

It was another providence that showed that the Lord wanted a prayer ministry in the conference. The date was set for the opening prayer conference. I was excited and the conference leadership and members were excited to hear and see how the Lord was about to fulfill His promise to pour out His Spirit on His repentant church.

The meeting was packed, which made Satan very angry. Yet, his power over the conference was broken. He was relentless in attempting to instill doubt and discouragement in me during those three days. I was bombarded with unholy thoughts and fears. Paul reminds us, "For we do not wrestle against flesh and blood, but against principalities, against powers, against the rulers of the darkness of this age, against spiritual hosts of wickedness in the heavenly places" (Eph. 6:12).

Satan and his demonic supernatural agencies were at war with me that day. I was petrified and prayed unceasingly until I was delivered from my fear. There was war in the meeting that weekend. The Bible states, "And war broke out in heaven: Michael and his angels fought with the dragon; and the dragon and his angels fought, but they did not prevail, nor was a place found for them in heaven any longer" (Rev. 12:7, 8). Pastor Telemaque was also attacked, losing his voice during the Friday evening presentation. He told us that he had never lost his voice during a prayer convocation before. We prayed, and his voice was restored. Praise God for prevailing prayers! The meeting continued with much prayer and thanksgiving.

A special highlight of the weekend was when Pastor Telemaque placed Conference President Willie Taylor in the middle of a circle, and pastors, prayer warriors, and members laid hands on him, petitioning heaven on his behalf and on behalf of his family and the conference. Pastor Telemaque declared, "An old era of a prayerless conference has ended, and a new era of a powerful praying conference and a "house of prayer for all nations" has begun.

The president thanked the Holy Spirit for allowing an ordinary member of the conference to relay a message to him to start this ministry. Immediately after he identified me as the channel the Holy Spirit used for that important message, Pastor Telemaque said: "Sister Turner will be going with me to a prayer conference in England."

This was the first time I had met Pastor Telemaque, and I thought, *Me? England? A prayer conference?*

I was frightened. I did not want to stop the blessings, for God's Word says: "Now it shall come to pass, if you diligently obey the voice of the LORD your God, to observe carefully all His commandments which I command you today, that the LORD your God will set you high above all nations of the earth. And all these blessings shall come upon you and overtake you, because you obey the voice of the LORD your God'" (Deut. 28:1, 2).

In humility and with much honor, praise, and thanksgiving to God, I accepted the invitation. I did not want to miss out on God's blessings, for I wanted to be overtaken by them. That is how I came to attend the prayer conference. The following year, I was asked to be a presenter. I attended the prayer conferences three years in succession and introduced "Praying Moms International." Many lives have been blessed.

Before Jesus left His disciples, He prepared them to be His witnesses, giving them the Great Commission, which calls for the preaching of the gospel in all the world. The task was greater than their own strength. Therefore, Jesus promised to send them the Holy Spirit who would guide and direct them in their being His witnesses. "But you shall receive power when the Holy Spirit has come upon you; and you shall be witnesses to Me in Jerusalem, and in all Judea and Samaria, and to the end of the earth" (Acts 1:8).

After praying for ten days in the upper room, they were filled with the Holy Spirit. Acts 1:14 records: "These all continued with one accord in prayer and supplication, with the women and Mary the mother of Jesus, and with His brothers." Acts 2:42 says: "And they continued steadfastly in the apostles' doctrine and fellowship, in the breaking of bread, and in prayers." Prayer empowered the apostolic church. They would never have survived without fervent prayer to God. They prayed for the presence of the Holy Spirit in times of opposition to the gospel. They prayed for Paul and the Ephesian elders, for Paul and Silas in the Philippian dungeon, and for the imprisoned Peter. They prayed for healing, and they prayed on many other occasions. The words "pray," "prayer," "prayers," "prayed," and "praying" are found thirty-two times in the book of Acts. Prayer was the focus of the early church.

What role did prayer play in the early Advent Movement? Ellen White participated in many of the early meetings in the years after the disappointment, and she answers this question.

> At our important meetings, these men [early Adventist leaders] would meet together and search for the truth as for hidden treasure. I met with them, and we studied and prayed earnestly; for we felt that we must learn God's truth. Often we remained together until late at night, and sometimes through the entire night, praying for light and studying the Word. As we fasted and prayed, great power came upon us. (Lt. 253, 1903, in *Manuscript Releases*, vol. 3, p. 413)

She brings forward the necessity of prayer:

> We must be much in prayer if we would make progress in the divine life. When the message of truth was first proclaimed, how much we prayed. How often was the voice of intercession heard in the chamber, in the barn, in the orchard, or the grove. Frequently we spent hours in earnest prayer, two or three together claiming the promise; often the sound of weeping was

heard and then the voice of thanksgiving and the song of praise. Now the day of God is nearer than when we first believed, and we should be more earnest, more zealous, and fervent than in those early days. Our perils are greater now than then. Souls are more hardened. We need now to be imbued with the spirit of Christ, and we should not rest until we receive it. (*Testimonies for the Church*, vol. 5, pp. 161, 162)

The biblical foundation of prayer and the wise counsel from Ellen White are the reasons the Holy Spirit led in the formation of a prayer ministry in this conference. The Lord called and anointed this conference to return to prayer as practiced in the apostolic church and in the early Advent Movement—a movement whose mission continues to be the depopulation of hell by the storming of the windows of heaven in prayer.

Since the inception of the prayer ministry, there has been a yearly convocation. Members have prayerfully opened their hearts and minds to the mission of the church. A spirit of true revival permeates the conference. Each member realizes that true revival always begins with one person—himself or herself—on his or her knees, crying out to the Lord.

The primary presenter at the convocation was Pastor Telemaque. He has trained thousands of prayer warriors and prayer coordinators how to run a successful "prayer room" during evangelistic meetings. He explains: "The primary function of the prayer room is to increase the visitors' receptivity to the gospel through Bible reading, confession of sins, faith in the divine power, supplication, and thanksgiving. To increase the visitors' receptivity to the gospel through the ministry of prayer is a process."

This process includes seven steps to be completed in seven minutes. They are:

1. The time the visitors arrive
2. Key question to visitors
3. Bible reading

4. Prayer of forgiveness
5. Prayer of faith
6. Prayer of supplication
7. Prayer of thanksgiving.

He also described seeing thousands of people come to Christ in baptism through prayer, the Holy Spirit, and the preaching of the Word. He asserted that, if you want to see a large movement of people coming to Christ in baptism, there must first be a movement of intercessory prayer at each local church and evangelistic meeting. "Prayer is evangelism, and evangelism is prayer," he said.

As prayer coordinator of the church I attend, I have used these principles and have witnessed miracles and healing during evangelistic meetings. Lives have changed, and many souls have been baptized.

This "prayer room" format has been adopted and widely used in this conference, and its ministry has impacted the Southern Union and many other conferences as well. At a recent prayer conference on the Holy Spirit presented by Pastor Telemaque, a presenter from another conference said that she was inadvertently invited to the convocation by answering someone else's telephone. When others learned about her special invitation, they invited her to come forward and give her testimony.

She said that she had never experienced the presence and power of the Holy Spirit as she did at this convocation. She planned to return to her conference and replicate the principles on how to be filled with the Holy Spirit. She was awed by the presence of the Holy Spirit and the power of prayer in the prayer room. "Like the woman at the well," she would return to her conference and invite other members to "Come see the One I met—the Holy Spirit. He taught me all I needed to know to prepare for the second coming of Jesus."

This is a practical application of how the Holy Spirit works. He will place anyone anywhere anytime to fulfill His mission and to glorify His name.

One of the most phenomenal and immediate answers to prayer I have ever experienced happened at one of our annual prayer conferences. A demon-possessed young man was brought to the conference by his parents for prayer and deliverance. As he moved towards the altar, his eyes bulged, he growled, his gait was uneven, and his hands were clenched, ready to punch anyone who came close to him. When a member tried to hold his hand, she was immediately attacked by Satan and fell flat on her back. However, she was not injured. Several of the elders restrained the young man, and the congregation cried out to the Lord in prayer for his deliverance.

The young man was taken to a secure room, and the Holy Spirit chose specific pastors, elders, and prayer warriors to intercede on his behalf. Separate from the main event, they prayed and prayed. Finally, the young man returned to the main auditorium singing and praising God, clothed and in his right mind. Sounds of jubilation and praise filled the room—"Hallelujah! Thank You, Jesus! Praise the Lord!" There was not a dry eye in the building. We praised God for the miracle that occurred that morning. I thought back on the story of the demoniac that Jesus healed. I was awed that I had observed the mighty power of God healing this demon-possessed young man.

The effect and influence of the Holy Spirit in this conference has reverberated throughout the Southern Union and the North American Division. Many of the leading, powerful Seventh-day Adventist prayer leaders have made presentations at our annual prayer conferences. These have included Pastors Pavel Goia, Philip Samaan, and Dennis Smith, to name just a few.

The formation of the prayer ministry has solidified the conference's mission with that of the General Conference and the world church of "Going Forward on Our Knees." Many of our churches have participated in the world church's prayer initiatives. At our local church, we have participated in the "Annual Ten Days of Prayer," formally known as "Operation Global Rain."

The new conference prayer ministry director Mrs. Mithra Williams is convinced that, through prayer, the Conference will go deeper in seeking a closer relationship with God, Jesus, and the Holy Spirit. We began a prayer initiative and launched a prayer walk, with t-shirts sporting our slogan: "Take it to the Streets Prayer Ministry." All churches in the Conference were asked to participate. The objective was to have the entire conference praying for Florida in united prayer at the same time and day. Hundreds of lives were blessed.

Our local church, Lighthouse Seventh-day Adventist Church, participated. Over fifty members, including children, teens, adults, and seniors took part in this life-changing event. Members returned to the church, rejoicing and testifying about their experience. The young people were impacted the most. They praised God that God used them through prayer to be a blessing to others. One young adult testified: "I thought it would be the usual door-to-door event, so I was not very excited to attend the prayer walk. However, this time it was different. It was a blessing to me." Prior to the prayer walk, the prayer team prayed that God would bless and change lives. He did.

As members of the conference, we believe the words of Christ, "If two of you shall agree on earth as touching any thing that they shall ask, it shall be done for them of my Father which is in heaven. For where two or three are gathered together in my name, there am I in the midst of them" (Matt. 18:19, 20, KJV). Ellen White comments on united prayer: "The promise is made on condition that the united prayers of the church are offered, and in answer to those prayers there may be expected a power greater than that which comes in answer to private prayer. The power given will be proportionate to the unity of the members and their love for God and one another" (Letter 32, 1903, MR No. 748, "The Power of United Prayer").

Our conference is indeed a "house of prayer for all nations." Our membership represents over fifty nations.

CHAPTER 7

Learning Patience to be Patient

> But let patience have its perfect work, that you may
> be perfect and complete, lacking nothing.
> —James 1:4

Why did God choose patience to teach me the importance of fulfilling His will and purpose in my life?

To find the answer, let us define the word "patience." Dictionary.com defines "patience" as "the quality of being, as the bearing of provocation, annoyance, misfortune, or pain, without complaint, loss of temper, irritation, or the like." It is also "quiet, steady perseverance; even-tempered care; diligence: to work with patience."

The *Cambridge English Dictionary* defines "patience" as "the ability to wait or to continue doing something despite difficulties, or to suffer without complaining or becoming annoyed."

How would I manifest this quality during this difficult, painful, and tremendously stressful period of my life? How does the contemporary Christian worldview of obtaining patience compare with that of the Scriptures?

We live in a world in which instant gratification is the norm. We have instant coffee, instant tea, instant noodles, to name just a few examples. Although I was a Christian, my daughter's crisis plunged me into a stressful situation. I needed her disaster to be resolved *now, in real time, instantly!* I demanded instant patience from God.

There are certain contemporary Christian groups who preach that patience can be obtained instantly if we command and demand that God act immediately on our behalf. Some claim that, by praying, I should be able to cast out my demon of impatience and fix my daughter's problem immediately. In so doing, prayer becomes an ultimatum rather than a trusting, building relationship with God. And, rather than accept God's sovereignty, it anticipates confronting God and demanding that He answer my prayer right away because I am His child.

Others subscribe to the concept of "name it and claim it," which means that, as followers of Jesus, Christians have the right to command God "in the name of Jesus" and get instant patience. I nearly fell into this satanic trap as I dealt with my daughter's calamity. I wanted her to return to the university *now* so she would become "my daughter the physician" and I would have bragging rights about her academic achievements. However, God had a different plan for teaching me patience. It would be through trials and afflictions. He wanted to teach me the biblical principle of patience that my faith would be strengthened.

The following verses confirmed God's plan to teach me how to be patient in dealing with my child and with others. "Let love be without hypocrisy. Abhor what is evil. Cling to what is good. Be kindly affectionate to one another with brotherly love, in honor giving preference to one another; not lagging in diligence, fervent in spirit, serving the Lord; rejoicing in hope, patient in tribulation, continuing steadfastly in prayer" (Rom. 12:9–12).

I experienced trials that tested my faith and hope. He assured me with the promise, "Cast your burden on the LORD, and He shall sustain you; He shall never permit the righteous to be moved" (Ps. 55:22).

According to the Bible, we learn patience when we experience trials and tribulations. The apostle Paul confirmed this fact in Romans 5:3, 4: "And not only that, but we also glory in tribulations, knowing that tribulation produces perseverance [patience]; and perseverance, character; and character, hope." James made the same point, agreeing with Paul. "My brethren, count it all joy when you fall into various trials, knowing that the testing of your faith produces patience. But let patience have its perfect work, that you may be perfect and complete, lacking nothing" (James 1:2–4).

These two statements laid the foundation for me to understand how I was to learn patience and be patient during this tumultuous time of my life.

"How helpful were these verses?" you may ask.

They taught me that I cannot be strong in the Lord without trials. They helped me to realize that my trials create the patience I need for greater trials ahead. If I gain the victory over a simple test, then, I am assured that the Lord will be with me in greater tests. He has confirmed this through Isaiah 41:13: "For I, the LORD your God, will hold your right hand, saying to you, 'Fear not, I will help you.'" God is saying, *I am teaching you how to be patient*.

Ellen White was in total agreement: "Trials will come upon us all, but if we will bear them uncomplainingly, we shall develop patience, meekness, and long-suffering with joyfulness" (*Review and Herald*, Oct. 7, 1890).

The apostle James described the process of developing endurance. He stated that faith was necessary to learn how to be patient. I discovered that faith is an action word. I had to act on my faith that Jesus would guide, lead, and teach me how to have patience. In his epistle, James argued that faith controls the tongue. This small organ must be held in check if we are to gain the victory over temptation and the desire to lash out or get even. He stated that, if we control our tongue, we can be joyful in temptation and we can gain the victory while we are learning patience.

My desire to learn how to be patient was connected to learning to control my tongue that I might communicate effectively with my daughter.

How will she react to my words? I thought. *Will my words build her up or tear her down in this fragile state of her life? Will they cause her pain?*

I prayed and asked the Lord to let me speak words of love over her life—words that would build us both up for the kingdom. I acknowledged the psalmist's prayer in Psalm 141:3: "Set a guard, O LORD, over my mouth; keep watch over the door of my lips." I also followed Paul's counsel in Ephesians 4:29: "Let no corrupt word proceed out of your mouth, but what is good for necessary edification, that it may impart grace to the hearers." The psalmist encouraged me in Psalm 37:7: "Rest in the LORD, and wait patiently for Him …" I gained the victory and learned how to be patient by practicing these verses daily.

As the trials intensified, I likened myself to a "diamond in the rough" and the afflictions I was experiencing, to the process by which carbon is transformed into a diamond. Common carbon is placed under intense heat and pressure for a long time. Finally, after this intense heat and pressure, a rough diamond is produced. A valuable gem, it can be worth millions of dollars. Likewise, the Lord uses the same process with me so that I can develop patience and become one of His precious jewels. The apostle Paul declared: "And we know that all things work together for good to those who love God, to those who are the called according to His purpose" (Rom. 8:28). Ellen White declares in *The Ministry of Healing*, p. 489, "All our sufferings and sorrows, all our temptations and trials, all our sadness and griefs, all our persecutions and privations, in short, all things work together for our good."

In my trials, God taught me how to learn patience to be patient. This lesson was a turning point in my relationship with the Lord and with my daughter. As the trials mounted and the tests intensified, I became stronger, more patient, and more useful in God's service. I was asked to serve as the prayer coordinator for my church and as an adult Sabbath

> **In my trials, God taught me how to learn patience to be patient.**

School teacher. As I studied the word, I was more patient with my daughter and with others. One young adult member exclaimed, "I like the new Sister Turner." God's plan became more evident in my life, and I refused to complain about my trials. I asked the Lord to let me bear them without complaint.

Ellen White explained: "Trials will come upon us all, but if we will bear them uncomplainingly, we shall develop patience, meekness, and longsuffering with joyfulness" (*Review and Herald*, October 7, 1890).

The difficult question remained: How do I experience joyfulness when my beloved child is making poor choices?

In answer, the Bible became my guide. I have learned that trials in my life produce patience, joy, and love. I needed these virtues to deal with the various issues that would arise. The psalmist encouraged me in Psalm 27:14 to—"Wait I say on the LORD: be of good courage, and He shall strengthen your heart; wait, I say, on the LORD!" He spoke to me through Habakkuk 2:3: "For the vision is yet for an appointed time; but at the end it will speak, and it will not lie. Though it tarries, wait for it; because it will surely come, it will not tarry." The Lord told me through 1 Corinthians 13:4: "Love suffers long." That means that love is patient.

I began demonstrating these virtues in my actions. I left love notes, cards, and flowers on her bed. She was delighted. My patience with her was the manifestation of my love for her. I reminded her that I would never stop loving her. The apostle John declares in 1 John 4:7: "Beloved, let us love one another, for love is of God; and everyone who loves is born of God and knows God."

By studying the Scriptures, it became real to me that I could not be strong in the Lord without trials. Crisis produces patience, discipline, and courage. These are Christian characteristics that I needed for the greater trials ahead and for my daughter to see Christ in me. Afflictions would either make me bitter or better. The apostle Paul reminded me in Hebrews 12:5, 6: "My son, do not despise the chastening of the LORD, nor be discouraged when you are rebuked by Him; for whom the LORD loves He chastens, and scourges every son whom He receives." This reminder told me that I am a beloved daughter of God who is blessed to be disciplined so that I can have a deeper relationship with my heavenly Father and with my daughter.

Ellen White wrote that God "permits temptations, trials, and afflictions to come to His loved ones. They are His providences, visitations of mercy to bring them back when they stray from His side, and give them a deeper sense of His presence and providential care. The peace that passeth understanding is not for those who shrink from trials, from struggles, and from self-denial" (*Our High Calling*, p. 327).

The Lord was working to resolve my crisis. However, Satan was not ready for God to work in either of our lives. He accused God of not solving my problems immediately. He whispered in my ear, "If God is so loving and merciful, why is He letting you suffer so long?" He accused me of growing weary and not having spiritual stamina: "You cannot have these problems resolved, for your faith is not strong," he taunted, "You are too weak for the long journey. How long have you been praying for your daughter's healing?"

Yet, the Lord intervened, overruling the devil's taunts and mockery. He reminded me that He was walking the journey with me and that He had gone before me: "… let us lay aside every weight, and the sin which so easily ensnares us, and let us run with endurance the race that is set before us, looking unto Jesus, the author and finisher of our faith, who for the joy that was set before Him endured the cross, despising the shame, and has sat down at the right hand of the throne of God" (Heb. 12:1, 2).

I was determined to press on in faith and in hope. As the Lord guided me, I developed spiritual stamina for the journey. I agree with Ellen White, when she wrote: "Men of stamina are wanted, men who will not wait to have their way smoothed and every obstacle removed, men who will inspire with fresh zeal the flagging efforts of dispirited workers, men whose hearts are warm with Christian love and whose hands are strong to do their Master's work" (*The Ministry of Healing*, p. 497).

I decided, by God's grace, to continue the race until victory was won. I continued to study the Bible, and I found in Hebrews, chapter 11, a partial list of successful and accomplished runners: Abraham, Abel, Enoch, Sarah, Isaac, Jacob, Joseph, and Moses. They ran a race of patience that was linked to their faith. Through their faith, they gained the victory. Their voices echoed in my ear, as they cheered me on. By the grace of God, we had faith and patience and we completed our journey. He will guide you. Run the race patiently. There is a great reward at the end. Through my faith, I too gained the victory. Hebrews 11:6 declares: "But without faith it is impossible to please Him, for he who comes to God must believe that He is, and that He is a rewarder of those who diligently seek Him." And, though they have won the victory, they have not yet received the prize. We will all receive the prize together—a crown and a harp—and we will all live together with Jesus for eternity. I will fight on till the victory is won and I see the King of kings.

I have a vision of God's future glory. There will be no more trials, no more tribulation, no more sorrows or tears, no more tauntings by Satan, and no more broken relationships. This promise filled my heart with joy, love, and peace. The battle is over. My daughter and I are victorious. We are in the presence of the great Overcomer. He has kept His promise in John 16:33: "These things I have spoken to you, that in Me you may have peace. In the world you will have tribulation; but be of good cheer, I have overcome the world."

Ellen White shared an inspiring thought about victory over trials and tribulations and the role that patience plays in the victor's life. "Soon the battle will have been fought, the victory won. Soon we shall see Him in whom our hopes of eternal life are centered. And in His presence the trials and sufferings of this life will seem as nothingness. The former things 'shall not be remembered, nor come into mind'" (*Prophets and Kings*, p. 731).

In Revelation 21:4, John the Revelator echoed that same thought: "And God will wipe away every tear from their eyes; there shall be no more death, nor sorrow, nor crying. There shall be no more pain, for the former things have passed away."

I experienced trials that tested my faith and hope. These were carefully controlled by God to teach me the precious virtue of patience in dealing with my child and with others. I cast all my burdens on Him. I surrendered fully to His chastening. I was blessed to know that God, in His wisdom, used my trials to teach me how to be patient.

I agree with what Ellen White wrote in *Our High Calling*, p. 318: "All trials, all afflictions, all peace, all safety, health, hope, life, and success are in God's hands, and He can control them all for the good of His children. It is our privilege to be suppliants, to ask anything of God, submitting our request in submission to His wise purposes and infinite will."

The apostle James summed it up this way: "Be patient therefore, brethren, unto the coming of the Lord. Behold, the husbandman waiteth for the precious fruit of the earth, and hath long patience for it, until he receives the early and latter rain. Be ye also patient; stablish you hearts: for the coming of the Lord draweth nigh" (James 5:7, 8, KJV).

CHAPTER 8

What is Intercessory Prayer?

So it was, when I heard these words, that I sat down and wept, and mourned for many days; I was fasting and praying before the God of heaven. And I said: "I pray, LORD God of heaven, O great and awesome God, You who keep Your covenant and mercy with those who love You and observe Your commandments, please let Your ear be attentive and Your eyes open, that You may hear the prayer of Your servant which I pray before You now, day and night, for the children of Israel Your servants, and confess the sins of the children of Israel which we have sinned against You. Both my father's house and I have sinned. We have acted very corruptly against You, and have not kept the commandments, the statutes, nor the ordinances which You commanded Your servant Moses.

Remember, I pray, the word that You commanded Your servant Moses, saying, 'If you are unfaithful, I will scatter you among the nations; but if you return to Me, and keep My

commandments and do them, though some of you were cast out to the farthest part of the heavens, yet I will gather them from there, and bring them to the place which I have chosen as a dwelling for My name.' Now these are Your servants and Your people, whom You have redeemed by Your great power, and by Your strong hand. O Lord, I pray, please let Your ear be attentive to the prayer of Your servant, and to the prayer of Your servants who desire to fear Your name; and let Your servant prosper this day, I pray, and grant him mercy in the sight of this man." For I was the king's cupbearer.
—Nehemiah 1:4–11

Intercessory prayer is the act of praying on behalf of others. An intercessor pleads another's case and takes that burden to the Lord. Intercessory prayer operates in the context of conflict, and it gives God absolute permission to exercise His power and intervene on another person's behalf.

The Biblical Foundation of Intercessory Prayer

What is the biblical foundation for intercessory prayer? The role of the intercessor or mediator is prevalent throughout Scripture. Some of the great intercessors of the Old Testament are Abraham, Moses, David, Daniel, Samuel, Hezekiah, Elijah, Jeremiah, Ezekiel, and Nehemiah. They all interceded on behalf of their people as they were confronted with tremendous challenges and conflicts.

Two of my favorite women intercessors are Hannah and Esther. Of the two, Hannah is my favorite. She is an encouragement to every woman and especially to mothers. The Bible relates her remarkable intercessory prayer and her joyful response after her prayer was answered. She felt overwhelmed in not being able to bear a child. She interceded passionately with God. Then she went to the temple and uttered a silent prayer. "Hannah spoke in her heart; only her lips moved, but her voice was not heard"

(1 Sam. 1:13). Eli the priest thought that she was drunk and rebuked her. Hannah told him about her anguish in being childless. Eli responded, "Go in peace, and the God of Israel grant your petition which you have asked of Him" (1 Sam. 1:17).

Hannah went back home. In the process of time, she was able to conceive and bore a son, whom she named "Samuel." Second Samuel, chapter 2, records her joyous response to her answered prayer. This is a chapter of thanksgiving and praise to God for answered prayers.

Like Hannah, I always respond with thanksgiving and praise for God's answers to my prayers. Even, when God, in His providence, does not answer my prayers as I desire, I still thank Him. Paul agrees in Philippians 4:6, "Be anxious for nothing, but in everything by prayer and supplications, with thanksgiving let your request be made known to God."

God called upon Esther to intercede on behalf of the Jewish nation to prevent their annihilation.

Paul and Peter are two of the great intercessors of the New Testament. However, the greatest of all intercessors is Jesus. The Bible records in Hebrews 7:25: "Therefore He is also able to save to the uttermost those who come to God through Him, since He always lives to make intercession for them."

The Old Testament understanding of the Levitical priesthood is the foundation for intercessory prayer. The priests' responsibility was to stand between God and sinful men, interceding on their behalf and offering sacrifices. The blood that was shed symbolized the forgiveness of sins and the acceptance of their prayers at the altar of incense. That symbolic service pointed to Jesus who died on the cross. His death changed the role of the Levitical priest.

Jesus our Model Intercessor

What was Jesus' role as He came to this sin-cursed world, and what is His role in heaven right now? Isaiah wrote: "He saw that there was no man, and wondered that there was no intercessor; therefore His own arm brought salvation for Him; and His own righteousness, it sustained Him" (Isa. 59:16). Jesus came to save sinful humankind and to restore human beings into perfect relationship with His Father.

His greatest intercession is recorded in John 17. Here He interceded with His Father to glorify Him as the Son, to preserve the disciples in unity and truth, and to glorify the disciples and all believers with Him in heaven. This includes *all* who are reading this book.

This prayer was not sufficient to complete the role that He came to fulfill. What else was required to accomplish this great task? John 12:32 answers: "And I, if I am lifted up from the earth, will draw all peoples to Myself."

As Jesus was nailed to the cruel cross and lifted up toward the sky, He hung between heaven and earth, between sinful man and a perfect God and a perfect heaven. He declared, as the model intercessor, in Luke 23:34: "Father, forgive them, for they do not know what they do."

Ellen White comments, "With amazement the angels beheld the infinite love of Jesus, who, suffering the most intense agony of mind and body, thought only of others, and encouraged the penitent soul to believe. In His humiliation He as a prophet had addressed the daughters of Jerusalem; as priest and advocate He had pleaded with the Father to forgive His murderers; as a loving Saviour He had forgiven the sins of the penitent thief" (*The Desire of Ages*, p. 752). The penitent thief represents all who ask for forgiveness.

After His resurrection, Jesus' role as Mediator and Intercessor continued in heaven. At the present time, His work of intercession is not yet complete. He stands before God on behalf of sinful men. The Bible confirms this fact. "For there is one God and one Mediator [Intercessor] between God and men, the Man Christ Jesus" (1 Tim. 2:5). "It is Christ that died, yea rather, that is risen again, who is even at the right hand of God, who also maketh intercession for us" (Rom. 8:34, KJV).

Who Should We Intercede For?

The Bible records those for whom we should intercede and for what purposes. What follows is a partial list of things mentioned in Scripture that we should pray for:

- Job 42:8 – Our friends
- Psalm 122:6 – The peace of Jerusalem
- Isaiah 49:25 – Our children
- Matthew 5:44 – Those who persecute us
- Matthew 9:36 – That laborers will be sent into God's harvest
- Luke 9:36 – That we enter not into temptation
- Romans 10:1 – That Israel may be saved
- 1 Timothy 2:1, 2 – Kings and for all those in authority
- James 5:14 – The sick.

A Model of Intercessory Prayer

God's People Must Pray Like Nehemiah

The trials and tribulations that I endured made me a woman of prayer. Jesus was my preferred intercessor. As I prayed and studied the Bible, the Lord answered my prayers with scriptures. Nehemiah became one of my favorite intercessors. That is why I included the long opening scripture from Nehemiah at the beginning of this chapter. The Lord used Nehemiah's model of intercession to teach me how to pray effectively.

Under the heading: **"Nehemiah's Prayer is an Example to God's People Today,"** Ellen White's book on prayer says:

> The hearts of those who advocate this cause must be filled with the Spirit of Jesus. The Great Physician alone can apply the balm of Gilead. Let these men [and women] read the book

of Nehemiah with humble hearts touched by the Holy Spirit, and their false ideas will be modified, and correct principles will be seen, and the present order of things will be changed. Nehemiah prayed to God for help, and God heard his prayer. The Lord moved upon heathen kings to come to his help. When his enemies zealously worked against him, the Lord worked through kings to carry out His purpose, and to answer the many prayers which were ascending to Him for the help which they so much needed. (*Review and Herald*, March 23, 1911, in *Prayer*, pp. 147, 148)

The Lord heard my prayers. I prayed that my daughter would return to the university and complete her education. Although she was a gifted student and was listed in the "Who's Who of American High School Students," disaster had struck her. Like the locusts that attacked the land of Israel, my daughter's own pestilence had descended upon her and destroyed her love for academics. However, God was not finished with her. He moved upon the heart of a prestigious university to take a chance on her. Now she is on the dean's list and is excelling. She is eagerly anticipating graduation and the prospects of becoming a successful and contributing citizen.

Under the heading, "**Prayer Made Nehemiah's Faith and Courage Stronger**," Ellen White's book on prayer declares:

> Overwhelmed with sorrow, Nehemiah could neither eat nor drink; he "wept, and mourned days, and fasted." In his grief he turned to the divine Helper. "I ... prayed," he said, "before the God of heaven." Faithfully he made confessions of his sins and the sins of his people. ... As Nehemiah prayed, his faith and courage grew strong. His mouth was filled with holy arguments. (*Prophets and Kings*, p. 629, in *Prayer*, p. 148)

Prayer Made Nehemiah's Faith and Courage Stronger

Like Nehemiah, my faith and courage grew stronger the more I prayed. I wept, I mourned, I fasted periodically through the years for God to intervene in our lives. I poured out my soul to God on behalf of myself and my daughter. I purposed in my heart to live a holy life, and I prayed that God would fill my mouth with holy arguments. He did. The psalmist reminds us in Psalm 19:14: "Let the words of my mouth and the meditation of my heart be acceptable in Your sight, O LORD, my strength and my Redeemer." I developed the pattern of not engaging in negative talk with my daughter.

One day she said something to me that made me realize that she was observing my actions: "Mom, you don't have to be a Christian every day." Praise God for holy arguments and a holy life! Ellen White agreed with maintaining biblical consistency all the time. "Christianity is not to be merely paraded on the Sabbath and displayed in the sanctuary; it is for every day in the week and for every place. Its claims must be recognized and obeyed in the workshop, at home, and in the business transactions with brethren and with the world" (*Testimonies for the Church*, vol. 4, p. 494, in *Conflict and Courage*, p. 119).

Nehemiah acknowledged his personal sins in his prayers. Ellen White wrote:

> Not only did Nehemiah say that Israel had sinned. He acknowledged with penitence that he and his father's house had sinned. "We have dealt corruptly against Thee," he says, placing himself among those who had dishonored God by not standing stiffly for the truth.... Nehemiah humbled himself before God,

giving Him the glory due to His name. Thus also did Daniel in Babylon. Let us study the prayers of these men. They teach us that we are to humble ourselves, but that we are never to obliterate the line of demarcation between God's commandment-keeping people and those who have no respect for the law. (Ms. 58, 1903, in *The Seventh-day Adventist Bible Commentary*, vol. 3, p. 1136)

Confess Your Sins

In a similar way, I recognized and acknowledged my sins and the sins of my family. I agonized with the Lord for forgiveness. I prayed about the sins that might have been passed down to me and my daughter, sins that might be considered generational curses. I humbled myself before God and asked Him to wipe out my transgression in dishonoring Him by breaking His commandments. "Against You, You only, have I sinned, and done this evil in Your sight" (Ps. 51:4), I cried, but He said to me, "My grace is sufficient for you, for My strength is made perfect in weakness" (2 Cor. 12:9). I accepted the gift of God's grace because God stands behind every promise He makes.

Under the heading, "**Nehemiah Prayed, Certain that God Would Fulfill His Promises**," Ellen White wrote:

> By faith taking fast hold of the divine promise, Nehemiah laid down at the footstool of heavenly mercy his petition that God would maintain the cause of His penitent people, restore their strength, and build up their waste places. God had been faithful to His threatenings when His people separated from Him; He had scattered them abroad among the nations, according to His Word. And Nehemiah found in this very fact an assurance that He would be equally faithful in fulfilling His promises.

(*Southern Watchman*, March 1, 1904, in *The Seventh-day Adventist Bible Commentary*, vol. 3, p. 1136)

God Certainly Fulfills His Promises

I prayed in a similar fashion, certain that God would fulfill His promise to restore my daughter and me back into His grace. Yet, He chose to scatter us among friends and family. During my trials and tribulations, it seemed as if I had been exiled to a strange, drought-filled country, and, like the prodigal in Jesus' parable, my daughter had gone into a far country and squandered her time and money. Unlike the parable, however, before she came home, God had to work on me first. He transformed my life, making me a woman of prayer and influencing and affecting the lives of many mothers and other women at the same time. He did the same for Israel in exile, guiding the lives of the Israelites while they were in a far country. He promised me, through His promise in Isaiah 58:11, 12: "The LORD will guide you continually, and satisfy your soul in drought, and strengthen your bones; you shall be like a watered garden, and like a spring of water, whose waters do not fail. Those from among you shall build the old waste places; you shall raise up the foundations of many generations; and you shall be called the Repairer of the Breach, the Restorer of Streets to Dwell in." He worked on me first. He transformed me into a woman of prayer who trusted the Holy Spirit to lead in her life. He allowed me to influence and affect the lives of many other women, especially mothers.

He promised to restore my daughter. He declared in Jeremiah 31:16, 17: "Refrain your voice from weeping, and your eyes from tears; for your work shall be rewarded, says the LORD, and they shall come back from the land of the enemy. There is hope in your future, says the LORD, that your children shall come back to their own border."

For Israel, He also promised to build up the waste places, including the Sabbath, which they had trampled on.

> Those from among you shall build the old waste places; you shall raise up the foundations of many generations; and you shall be called the Repairer of the Breach, the Restorer of Streets to Dwell In. "If you turn away your foot from the Sabbath, from doing your pleasure on My holy day, and call the Sabbath a delight, the holy day of the LORD honorable, and shall honor Him, not doing your own ways, nor finding your own pleasure, nor speaking your own words, then you shall delight yourself in the LORD; and I will cause you to ride on the high hills of the earth, and feed you with the heritage of Jacob your father. The mouth of the LORD has spoken." (Isa. 58:11–14)

I have now turned away my foot from trampling on the Sabbath and doing my own pleasure. The Sabbath is a delight to me. I worship, honor, and adore the Lord on His holy day.

A friend had observed my relationship with God by the way I observed the Sabbath. She wanted me to be the mistress of ceremonies at her retirement. However, she knew that I would not be able to attend the function at midday on a Saturday. Though luncheons are much cheaper than dinners, she changed the time from noon to after sunset to accommodate the Lord's Sabbath, for which I honored and glorified God's name. First Corinthians 10:31 says: "Therefore, whether you eat or drink, or whatever you do, do all to the glory of God."

Ellen White exhorted: "There is need of Nehemiahs in the church today,—not men who can pray and preach only, but men whose prayers and sermons are braced with firm and eager purpose" (*Signs of the Times*, Dec. 6, 1883). Although I am not a preacher, my life became a sermon to my daughter. I purposed in my heart that my prayer life would be purposeful. My prayer commitment was that God would be the center of my prayers and that the focus of my prayers would be my relationship with God. This commitment motivated me to build a forever friendship with God Himself, with His Son Jesus, and with the Holy Spirit.

Each member of the heavenly Trio had a different function in my prayer life (*Heavenly Places*, p. 336). The Holy Spirit brought conviction to me about my sins. "And when He has come, He will convict the world of sin, and of righteousness, and of judgment" (John 16:8). He also brought me to Jesus. Then, Jesus brought me to His Father. "No one can come to Me unless the Father who sent Me draws him" (John 6:44). All three worked together to enable me to become an overcomer. They also transformed my daughter's life.

Like Nehemiah, we can pray at any time or place.

> To pray as Nehemiah prayed in his hour of need is a resource at the command of the Christian under circumstances when other forms of prayer may be impossible. Toilers in the busy walks of life, crowded and almost overwhelmed with perplexity, can send up a petition to God for divine guidance. Travelers by sea and land, when threatened with some great danger, can thus commit themselves to Heaven's protection. In times of sudden difficulty or peril the heart may send up its cry for help to One who has pledged Himself to come to the aid of His faithful, believing ones whenever they call upon Him. In every circumstance, under every condition, the soul weighed down with grief and care, or fiercely assailed by temptation, may find assurance, support, and succor in the unfailing love and power of a covenant-keeping God.
>
> Nehemiah, in that brief moment of prayer to the King of kings, gathered courage to tell Artaxerxes of his desire to be released for a time from his duties at the court, and he asked for authority to build up the waste places of Jerusalem and to make it once more a strong and defensed city. Momentous results to the Jewish nation hung upon this request. "And," Nehemiah declares, "the king granted me, according to the good hand of my God upon me." (*Prophets and Kings*, pp. 631, 632)

Pray at Anytime or Place

I have prayed and interceded in various places and under varied circumstances. I have prayed in my car, at home, and at church, and I have prayed wherever the Holy Spirit has prompted me to pray. At my staff meetings, when the team became uncivil, I prayed silently, asking the Lord to take control and restore calm and order. Immediately, everyone was calm. Miracles have happened when I pray in these difficult and critical times.

> I have prayed and interceded in various places and under varied circumstances.

Prayer Walking

Prayer walking is another method of praying that I have used. I walk through different neighborhoods, in the marketplace and schools, reaching out and interceding for the community.

When I walk and pray, I ask the Lord to send someone for me to witness to. He always does. One year the Holy Spirit instructed me to start handing out tracts to all the walkers on the trail I regularly hiked. That year I distributed over five hundred "Glow Tracts" to the "winter birds," the Canadians who spend winters in sunny Florida. Several engaged me in conversation after receiving a tract. One particular favorite tract was, "Why I go to church on Saturday." To many who received this tract it seemed a strange day to go to church. Two of the visitors and I became friends. I wanted them to get to know Jesus as I knew Him.

One commented: "Do you know that you give away something every day?"

It was true that I distributed tracts every day. However, I was not aware that anyone would have noted the fact.

"If you read these tracts you will have eternal life," I replied.

These men became my friends. They told their wives about "the woman who walks by the lake, prays for them on the trail, gives them tracts, and preaches to them." I met their wives and over fifty other visitors when they invited me to their "returning home party." One of the wives told me, "You are doing a good job; they need to be converted."

At the party, my new friend invited me to tell the group what I do when I walk the trail. I shared my faith with them and talked about God's goodness. I asked if I could pray for the safe travel of the group as they returned to Canada. I thank God for allowing me to meet and socialize with my new Catholic friends on the trail.

I was also able to witness to them about God's health plan by informing them that I do not use stimulants such as alcohol, tobacco, or coffee. They respected my convictions and offered me water instead. Several of the ladies volunteered to give me clothes that they would not be taking back with them. I collected several large bags of these and distributed them to the needy.

The following year my friends returned. One was very excited when he saw me. "I have some very good news for you."

"What is the good news?" I asked excitedly.

"I am reading the Bible," he said, beaming with joy. He had never read the Bible before I encouraged him to do so. However, Satan was not ready to release him. His priest told him not to read the Bible. He said, "Read ours instead."

"I am determined to read the Bible," he responded, knowing that he had found new treasure.

I enjoyed these blessings because I dared to prayer walk and distribute tracts. I thank God that He put someone in my path to pray for and witness to.

Pray Without Ceasing—Anytime, Anywhere

Nehemiah prayed earnestly all night.

> In secrecy and silence, Nehemiah completed his circuit of the walls. He declares, "The rulers knew not whither I went, or

what I did; neither had I as yet told it to the Jews, nor to the priests, nor to the nobles, nor to the rulers, nor to the rest that did the work." In this painful survey he did not wish to attract the attention of either friends or foes, lest an excitement should be created, and reports be put in circulation that might defeat, or at least hinder, his work. Nehemiah devoted the remainder of the night to prayer; in the morning there must be earnest effort to arouse and unite his dispirited and divided countrymen. —*The Southern Watchman*, March 22, 1904. (*Christian Service*, p. 174)

During the deepest, darkest hours of my afflictions and trials, I had only one recourse: *prayer!* My nights were filled with sorrow, worry, and tears until the master calmed my fears. He said: "Fear not, for I am with you; be not dismayed, for I am your God. I will strengthen you, yes, I will help you, I will uphold you with My righteous right hand" (Isaiah 41:10). He comforted me: "Peace I leave with you, My peace I give to you; not as the world gives do I give to you. Let not your heart be troubled, neither let it be afraid" (John 14:27). These were some of the comforting promises He gave to me as I agonized all night for myself and for my daughter.

I prayed like Jesus, who prayed all night when He had something important to accomplish like selecting His disciples (see Luke 6:12). Nehemiah also prayed all night when the fate of the nation was in jeopardy. My salvation and my daughter's salvation were under threat. I prayed all night. I was blessed and assured by the hopeful note of Psalm 30: "For His anger is but for a moment, His favor is for life; weeping may endure for a night, but joy comes in the morning" (Ps. 30:5). My joy did come in the morning when my daughter returned home safely. Ellen White described how Nehemiah's success shows the power of prayer:

> In their work, Ezra and Nehemiah humbled themselves before God, confessing their sins and the sins of their people, and entreating pardon as if they themselves were the offenders.

Patiently they toiled and prayed and suffered. That which made their work most difficult was not the open hostility of the heathen, but the secret opposition of pretended friends, who, by lending their influence to the service of evil, increased tenfold the burden of God's servants. These traitors furnished the Lord's enemies with material to use in their warfare upon His people. Their evil passions and rebellious wills were ever at war with the plain requirements of God.

The success attending Nehemiah's efforts shows what prayer, faith, and wise, energetic action will accomplish.... As he came into contact with evil and opposition to right he took so determined a stand that the people were roused to labor with fresh zeal and courage. They could not but recognize his loyalty, his patriotism, and his deep love for God; and, seeing this, they were willing to follow where he led. (*Prophets and Kings*, pp. 675, 676)

Ellen White's Comments on Intercessory Prayer

Ellen White, the world's most translated Christian writer, commented on the value of intercessory prayer.

In calling God our Father, we recognize all His children as our brethren. We are all a part of the great web of humanity, all members of one family. In our petitions we are to include our neighbors as well as ourselves. No one prays aright who seeks a blessing for himself alone. (*Sons and Daughters of God*, p. 267)

As we seek to win others to Christ, bearing the burden of souls in our prayers, our own hearts will throb with the quickening influence of God's grace; our own affections will glow with more divine fervor; our whole Christian life will be more of a reality, more earnest, more prayerful. (*Christ's Object Lessons*, p. 354)

Pray for Blessings to Bless Others

Our prayers are not to be a selfish asking, merely for our own benefit. We are to ask that we may give. The principle of Christ's life must be the principle of our lives. "For their sakes," He said, speaking of His disciples, "I sanctify Myself, that they also might be sanctified." John 17:19. The same devotion, the same self-sacrifice, the same subjection to the claims of the word of God, that were manifest in Christ, must be seen in His servants. Our mission to the world is not to serve or please ourselves; we are to glorify God by co-operating with Him to save sinners. We are to ask blessings from God that we may communicate to others. The capacity for receiving is preserved only by imparting. We cannot continue to receive heavenly treasure without communicating to those around us. (*Christ's Object Lessons*, pp. 142, 143)

Parents Are to Pray for Their Children

God has promised to give wisdom to those that ask in faith, and He will do just as He said He would. He is pleased with the faith that takes Him at His word. The mother of Augustine prayed for her son's conversion. She saw no evidence that the Spirit of God was impressing his heart, but she was not discouraged. She laid her finger upon the texts, presenting before God His own words, and pleaded as only a mother can. Her deep humiliation, her earnest importunities, her unwavering faith, prevailed, and the Lord gave her the desire of her heart. Today He is just as ready to listen to the petitions of His people. His "hand is not shortened, that it cannot save; neither His ear heavy, that it cannot hear;" and if Christian parents seek Him earnestly, He will fill their mouths with arguments, and for His name's sake will work mightily in their behalf in the conversion of their children. (*Testimonies for the Church*, vol. 5, pp. 322, 323)

Jesus is calling all Christians to become mighty intercessors. Ask the Holy Spirit to teach you how to pray. The disciples asked Jesus to teach them how to pray after they observed the power in His ministry, and, when He did, they experienced the power of intercessory prayer in their own ministries. The evidence of the power of intercessory prayer for the disciples was in the spreading of the gospel to the world after the day of Pentecost.

I encourage you to become an intercessor, and you will be a blessing to yourself and to others. All the while, your Father will be by your side, "bending over you with unutterable love, afflicting you for your good, as the refiner purifies the precious ore. When you have thought yourself forsaken, he has been near you to comfort and sustain" (*Gospel Workers*, p. 373).

Heaven is Opened to Every Mother's Prayer

When Christ bowed on the banks of Jordan after His baptism and offered up prayer in behalf of humanity, the heavens were opened; and the Spirit of God, like a dove of burnished gold, encircled the form of the Saviour; and a voice came from heaven which said, "This is my beloved Son, in whom I am well pleased."

What significance does this have for you? It says that heaven is open to your prayers. It says that you are accepted in the Beloved. The gates are open for every mother who would lay her burden at the Saviour's feet. It says that Christ has encircled the race with His human arm, and with His divine arm He has grasped the throne of the Infinite and united man with God, and earth with heaven. (*Child Guidance*, pp. 525, 526)

A Precious Privilege

This is an encouraging lesson for mothers, to mothers for all time. After they have done the best they can do for the good of their children, they may bring them to Jesus. Even the babes in the mother's arms are precious in His sight. And as the mother's heart yearns for the help she knows she cannot give, the grace she cannot bestow, and she casts herself and children into the merciful arms of Christ, He will receive and bless them; He will give peace, hope, and happiness to mother and children. This is a precious privilege which Jesus has granted to all mothers. (*Adventist Home*, p. 274)

Be Much in Secret Prayer

Did mothers but realize the importance of their mission, they would be much in secret prayer, presenting their children to Jesus, imploring His blessing upon them, and pleading for wisdom to discharge aright their sacred duties. Let the mother improve every opportunity to mold and fashion the disposition and habits of her children. Let her watch carefully the development of character, repressing traits that are too prominent, encouraging those that are deficient. Let her make her own life a pure and noble example to her precious charge.

The mother should enter upon her work with courage and energy, relying constantly upon divine aid in all her efforts. She should never rest satisfied until she sees in her children a gradual elevation of character, until they have a higher object in life than merely to seek their own pleasure. (*Adventist Home*, pp. 265, 266)

An Influence That Will Last Forever

The influence of a praying, God-fearing mother will last through eternity. She may die, but her work will endure. (*Testimonies for the Church*, vol. 4, p. 500)

Why Do I Intercede?

The Holy Spirit used my trials and afflictions as the channel to open doors for other grieving mothers and relatives who are searching for answers as to why their children have left the faith. The agony and trials that I have experienced with my daughter prepared me to minister to others by offering comfort and encouragement. If I had not experienced similar trials, I could not offer the help they needed.

During one presentation in England, mothers wept and nodded their heads in agreement with me as they identified with me in having the same trials as they had with their children. One mother shared the experience of awakening in the early morning to agonize and pray for her child. At that very moment, she learned, he had been attempting suicide. The Holy Spirit had intervened, and her child was saved. I reminded the mothers present that God has promised: "For I will contend with him who contends with you, and I will save your children.... All flesh shall know that I, the LORD, am your Savior, and your Redeemer, the Mighty One of Jacob" (Isa. 49:25, 26).

I persuaded them to continue to help other mothers under the inspired encouragement of Ellen White: "Those who have borne the greatest sorrows are frequently the ones who carry the greatest comfort to others, bringing sunshine wherever they go. Such ones have been chastened and sweetened by their afflictions; they did not lose confidence in God when trouble assailed them but clung closer to His protecting love. Such ones are living proof of the tender care of God who makes the darkness as well as the light and chastens us for our good" (*God's Amazing Grace*, p. 122).

Mrs. White also explained, "God permits trials to assail His people, that by their constancy and obedience they themselves may be spiritually enriched, and that their example may be a source of strength to others" (*Patriarchs and Prophets*, p. 129).

The Holy Spirit also reminded me: "The very trials that test our faith most severely, and make it seem that God has forsaken us, are designed to lead us nearer to Christ, that we may lay all of our burdens at his feet, and receive the peace he will give us in exchange.... When you surrender yourself entirely to God, when you fall all broken upon Jesus, you will be rewarded by a victory the joy of which you have never yet realized. As you review the past with a clear vision, you will see that at the very time when life seemed to you only a perplexity and a burden, Jesus himself was near you, seeking to lead you in the light. Your Father was by your side" (*Gospel Workers*, p. 372).

Intercessory prayer has become a passion in my life. I will continue to devote time to helping and teaching others to have the joy of communicating with God. The Bible is my textbook, and this is what it says about intercessory prayer:

"Praying always with all prayer and supplication in the Spirit, being watchful to this end with all perseverance and supplication for all the saints" (Eph. 6:18).

"Now this is the confidence that we have in Him, that if we ask anything according to His will, He hears us. And if we know that He hears us, whatever we ask, we know that we have the petitions that we have asked of Him" (1 John 5:14, 15).

CHAPTER 9

Before You Call I Will Answer

It shall come to pass that before they call, I will answer;
and while they are still speaking, I will hear.
—Isaiah 65:24

It was an absolutely glorious summer Sunday afternoon. The sun shone brightly. The sky was a clear blue.

Blue, I thought, as I reflected on the story in Numbers 15, where the Lord reminded the children of Israel "to make tassels on the corners of their garments" and "put a blue thread in the tassels ... that you may look upon it and remember all the commandments of the LORD" (Num. 15:38, 39).

"Please bring back the memory of commandment keeping and the love of Jesus to my daughter's mind," I prayed. Blue represents God's throne and His commandments. As I gazed on the blue sky and reflected on this passage, I longed for the days in which we both remembered God's love and grace towards us as we strolled leisurely in the park or on the beach.

We held hands, sang choruses and jingles. We thanked and praised the Lord for His goodness and mercies.

Jesus told His disciples, in John 14:15: "If you love me, keep My commandments." Ellen White reminds us, "There are many who, though striving to obey God's commandments, have little peace and joy. ... They walk as it were in a salt land, a parched wilderness. They claim little, when they might claim much; for there is no limit to the promise of God. Such ones do not correctly represent the sanctification that comes through obedience to the truth. The Lord would have all His sons and daughters happy, peaceful, and obedient. Through the exercise of faith the believer comes into the possession of these blessings. Through faith, every deficiency of character may be supplied, every defilement cleansed, every fault corrected, every excellence developed" (*The Acts of the Apostles*, p. 563). *Where is the love that we should be experiencing as mother and daughter?* I thought.

But these were only memories now. There is no more walking on the beach or picnics in the park or talking about God's love for us. My eyes were filled with tears as I remembered the love and great relationship we had enjoyed.

Serenity and peace were in the atmosphere. Harmony with God was evident. Birds fluttered from branch to branch, chirping merrily as they fed on the nectar of the flowers. They were very happy and seemed to be communing. One sang and then another echoed a response.

But there was no communion in my house. There was no one to talk to about the conflict and struggles I was experiencing with my only child. A painful breath-taking silence filled the house. The absentee father loomed heavily on my mind. *Would his presence have made a positive influence or a difference in my daughter's life? Would she have rebelled if he were an important person in her life?* I wondered.

I was reminded about the consequences of disobedience and sin. It was not God's plan that I should abandon my faith, the church, and the principles of the Holy Scripture to have a daughter outside of marriage.

I had been deceived by Satan. The world teaches that it is okay to have a child outside of wedlock if you can provide the finances necessary to support the child. Hollywood and the entertainment industry glorify the single parent choice, and I fell for it all. Popular morays about marriage are merely another assault on God's law. The perfect law of freedom provides freedom to choose.

The word of God is true and sure. I reflected on the wise man Solomon's summary of the meaning of life: "Let us hear the conclusion of the whole matter: Fear God and keep His commandments, for this is man's all. For God will bring every work into judgment, including every secret thing, whether good or evil" (Eccles. 12:14).

Pondering the poor choices I have made and how they have affected my child, I cannot help but thank God for His amazing grace, mercy, and protection. Likewise, I cannot help but thank Him for His promises in Isaiah 1:18, Ephesians 2:8, and Hebrews 13:5: "'Come let us reason together,' says the LORD, 'Though your sins be as scarlet they shall be as white as snow.'" "For by grace you have been saved through faith, and that not of yourselves; it is the gift of God." "I will never leave you nor forsake you."

> **Pondering the poor choices I have made and how they have affected my child, I cannot help but thank God for His amazing grace, mercy, and protection.**

Although I reveled in God's grace, mercies, and protection, my fears were compounded because I did not know where my teenage daughter was. With bitterness and anger I lashed out at God.

"Where is my child?" I yelled. "Please protect her from danger! How do I cope with this hopeless situation?"

Immediately I got a response. My fears and anxiety were calmed.

"Talk to Me since there is no one else to talk to."

Slowly and convincingly the Holy Spirit guided my thoughts to First John, chapter 3: "Behold what manner of love the Father has bestowed on us, that we should be called children of God.... Beloved, now we are children of God; and it has not yet been revealed what we shall be, but we know that when He is revealed, we shall be like Him, for we shall see Him as He is.... And you know that He was manifested to take away our sins" (1 John 3:1, 2, 5).

I repeated and clung to those promises. I continued to pray for the protection and safety of my only child. Ellen White wrote encouragingly:

> It is in these promises that Christ communicates to us His grace and power. They are leaves from that tree which is "for the healing of the nations." Revelation 22:2. Received, assimilated, they are to be the strength of the character, the inspiration and sustenance of the life. Nothing else can have such healing power. Nothing besides can impart the courage and faith which give vital energy to the whole being. (*The Ministry of Healing*, p. 122)

I needed immediate healing for my daughter and for myself. I pleaded with God to strengthen and sustain us. I received a command of assurance about the Father's love for me and my daughter. He would take away our sins. As I contemplated the words of the scripture given me, the Holy Spirit prompted me to pray and to cling to God's Word.

I was assured by the prophet, "For as the rain comes down, and the snow from heaven, and do not return there, but water the earth, and make it bring forth and bud, that it may give seed to the sower and bread to the eater, so shall My word be that goes forth from My mouth; it shall not return to Me void, but it shall accomplish what I please, and it shall prosper in the thing for which I sent it" (Isa. 55:10, 11). The Lord spoke to me through His Word. I accepted the promise that He gave me in this way.

Nonetheless, I yearned to experience the power of the full measure of the Holy Spirit in my life. I wanted a power that would turn my life into ministry for my daughter so that she could see Christ in me. The Holy Spirit had just spoken to me through His word. Now it was my turn to speak to Him through prayer. I wanted to talk to someone. The Creator was now giving me a very special and personal opportunity to talk to Him as a friend.

I prayed, humbling my heart, confessing every sin I could recall, and emptying my heart of every violation of God's will for me. I was deeply sorrowful for my sins and concerned how my sins might have affected my child. Yet, God's promise is; "If we confess our sins, He is faithful and just to forgive us our sins and to cleanse us from all unrighteousness" (1 John 1:9). The psalmist David echoed this plea in the fifty-first psalm: "Have mercy upon me, O God, according to Your lovingkindness; according to the multitude of Your tender mercies, blot out my transgressions. Wash me thoroughly from my iniquity, and cleanse me from my sin.... Purge me with hyssop, and I shall be clean; wash me, and I shall be whiter than snow.... Create in me a clean heart, O God, and renew a steadfast spirit within me.... Restore to me the joy of Your salvation, and uphold me by Your generous Spirit. Then I will teach transgressors Your ways, and sinners shall be converted to You" (Ps. 51:1, 2, 7, 10, 12, 13).

I pleaded with the Holy Spirit to open my heart that I might be more obedient and receptive to His promptings. Ellen White wrote: "The heart must be emptied of every defilement and cleansed for the indwelling of the Spirit. It was by confession and forsaking of sin, by earnest prayer and consecration of themselves to God, that the early disciples prepared for the outpouring of the Holy Spirit on the Day of Pentecost. The same work, only in a greater degree, must be done now" (*Testimonies to Ministers*, p. 507).

Regarding our need of the Holy Spirit, Ellen White wrote: "What we need is the baptism of the Holy Spirit. Without this, we are no more fitted to go forth to the world than were the disciples after the crucifixion of their Lord. Jesus knew their destitution, and told them to tarry in Jerusalem until they should be endowed with power from on high" (*Review and Herald*, Feb. 18, 1890).

"We should pray as earnestly for the descent of the Holy Spirit as the disciples prayed on the day of Pentecost. If they needed it at that time, we need it more today" (*Testimonies for the Church*, vol. 5, p. 158).

I continued praying. I asked the Lord to protect my daughter from the dangers of this dark world and to guide her. The night turned into morning; the morning turned into afternoon. I waited anxiously for my child to call or to come home. I continued praying passionately for her safety. Suddenly the front door opened.

"Thank You, Lord, for her safe return home!"

She went to her room without speaking and closed the door.

Rejected and saddened that she did not acknowledge me, I continued to pray, prostrating myself on the floor and pleading my case to the Lord again and again. I asked Him to heal a brokenhearted mother so that she could help her hurting child. The Lord reminded me—

"Do not be afraid ... for the battle is not yours, but God's" (2 Chron. 20:15). My heart was strengthened in knowing that God was fighting this battle for me. He also reminded me about Sarah who thought her desire to have a child was hopeless. He reminded Sarah—and He reminded me—in Genesis 18:14: "Is anything too hard for the Lord?"

The prayers continued. Immediately it appeared to me as if the roof of my daughter's room was opened and two beautiful angels dressed in white alighted on each side of her bed. They stretched their wings tip to tip, heads touching, encircling her and covering the entire bed. The angels lingered and breathed the breath of "the Almighty" on her. Job 33:4 declares: "The Spirit of God has made me, and the breath of the Almighty gives me life."

Consider Ellen White's comment about the ministry of angels:

> When Christ ascended to the Father, He did not leave His followers without help. The Holy Spirit, as His representative, and

the heavenly angels, as ministering spirits, are sent forth to aid those who against great odds are fighting the good fight of faith. Ever remember that Jesus is your helper.... Nothing is apparently more helpless, yet really more invincible, than the soul that feels its nothingness and relies wholly on the merits of the Saviour. God would send every angel in heaven to the aid of such a one, rather than allow him to be overcome. Angels are God's ministers, radiant with the light ever flowing from His presence, and speeding on rapid wing to execute His will. Angels are ever present where they are most needed, with those who have the hardest battle with self to fight, and whose surroundings are the most discouraging. (*Sons and Daughters of God*, p. 35)

Ministering angels are waiting about the throne to instantly obey the mandate of Jesus Christ to answer every prayer offered in earnest, living faith. (*Selected Message*, bk. 2, p. 377)

That afternoon, I witnessed the power and manifestation of those ministering angels in my house. I agree with Paul's question in Hebrews 1:14, "Are they not all ministering spirits sent forth to minister for those who will inherit salvation?"

I continued to agonize with God. A bright light flooded my daughter's room. It was God's glory. He had dispatched His angels in answer to my prayer. I continued to praise the Lord as the beautiful scene unfolded before me. The Spirit of God moved upon my daughter and transformed her, giving her a new life and light. Jesus said, "It is the Spirit who gives life" (John 6:63).

After a bit, she came out of her room and knocked on my door. She entered my room, smiling cheerfully, as if nothing had happened since I had last seen her two days before. I was still absorbed in silent prayer. The Spirit impressed on my mind the promise of Isaiah 65:24: "It shall come to pass that before they call, I will answer; and while they are still speaking, I will hear."

Yes, while I was speaking, God had answered my prayer.

"Mom, I am hungry. Can you fix dinner for me?" I got up and prepared the meal. I wanted her to know that, despite our challenges, I loved her dearly. I took Jesus' counsel seriously when He said, "And the King will answer and say to them, 'Assuredly, I say to you, inasmuch as you did it to one of the least of these My brethren, you did it to Me'" (Matt. 25:40). A hungry child needed physical, emotional, and spiritual food. I had a household responsibility to fulfill.

Note Ellen White's comment on our household responsibilities:

> Whenever you take up the duty that lies nearest you, then God will bless you, and hear your prayers. There are too many doing outside missionary work, while their own households are left destitute of any such efforts,—going to ruin through neglect.... The first missionary work is to see that love, light, and joy come into the home circle. Let us not be looking for some great temperance or missionary work to do until we have first done the duties at home. Every morning we should think, What kind act can I do today? What tender word can I speak? Kind words at home are blessed sunshine. (*Sons and Daughters of God*, p. 252)

Those were the questions I answered when I prepared the meal for my beloved child who did not acknowledge me after she returned from being gone for two days without communication.

Ellen White admonishes us:

> The life of Christ was an ever-widening, shoreless influence, an influence that bound Him to God and to the whole human family... Every soul is surrounded by an atmosphere of its own—an atmosphere, it may be, charged with the life-giving power of faith, courage, and hope, and sweet with the

fragrance of love.... By the atmosphere surrounding us, every person with whom we come in contact is consciously or unconsciously affected.

This is a responsibility from which we cannot free ourselves. Our words, our acts, our dress, our deportment, even the expression of the countenance, has an influence.

Upon the impression thus made there hang results for good or evil which no man can measure. Every impulse thus imparted is seed sown which will produce its harvest. It is a link in the long chain of human events, extending we know not whither. If by our example we aid others in the development of good principles, we give them power to do good. In their turn they exert the same influence upon others, and they upon still others. Thus by our unconscious influence thousands may be blessed. (*Christ's Object Lessons*, pp. 339, 340)

This very vivid encounter with God the Holy Spirit, in answering my prayer "while I was yet speaking," aroused a great feeling of excitement in my life about prayer and the Holy Spirit. It kindled a fire of a more passionate, radical, and bold prayer life that was to grow into a blaze. As the Holy Spirit guided, intercessory prayer became my passion.

Jesus the Word and the Holy Spirit set my life on fire for the Lord. I had an increasing appreciation for seeking the Lord on behalf of my child's salvation and that of all children.

CHAPTER 10

The Family Power-Packed Prayer Line

> If My people who are called by My name will humble
> themselves, and pray and seek My face, and turn from their
> wicked ways, then I will hear from heaven, and will forgive
> their sin and heal their land.
> —2 Chronicles 7:14

How do you deal with the grueling, grinding stress of life?

How do you cope with the mortgage rate, foreclosures, and unemployment?

How do you handle teen pregnancy?

How do you, as a couple faithful to each other, handle the inability to conceive even though you are married, have prayed and prayed for a child, and yet are still childless?

How do you interact with rebellious young people who spend every waking moment on social media?

How do you relate to the fact that thousands and even millions of people are abandoning their faith annually?

How do you handle the political crisis in your country and around the world?
Do you find these questions perplexing and too difficult to manage?
Are these problems in your life too difficult to answer?
Do you have a lifeline to help with these problems?
If not, why not?

Surely you are not the only one who has been confronted with baffling issues and situations. When the Lord visited Abraham and Sarah and told Sarah, who was advanced in age, that, at the appointed time, she would conceive and give birth to a child, she thought the prediction impossible and laughed. The Lord asked Abraham, "Why did Sarah laugh, saying 'Shall I surely bear a child, since I am old?'" (Gen. 18:13). Then the Lord issued a startling question, "Is anything too hard for the LORD?" (Gen. 18:14).

Sarah laughed because she forgot that the Creator, the sovereign Lord, was still in charge. At the appointed time, she gave birth to the child as the Lord had promised. Out of that lineage our Messiah, the Savior Jesus Christ, was born.

As we face our own challenges, the Lord is still asking the same question He asked Sarah, a question that He has also answered. "Casting all your care upon Him, for He cares for you" (1 Peter 5:7).

My family accepted the invitation to cast all our cares upon Him together the day we received devastating news. It was a Friday after midnight. After a Spirit-filled devotion, I had retired early to bed. My deep and peaceful sleep was interrupted by the loud ringing of the telephone. I was frightened. *It must be urgent*, I thought.

"Hello?"

The voice that responded to my greeting was that of my niece Carol. She was hysterical.

"We have an emergency. Cassandra called. Her brother Garfield has been diagnosed with stage four colon cancer. Everyone is distraught. He has all the classical signs and symptoms, severe weight loss, poor appetite, rectal bleeding, and a confirmed biopsy. Let's pray."

She connected as many family members as could be reached. We interceded passionately and fervently. We pleaded with the Lord, according to His will, to heal Garfield. We cried uncontrollably as we interceded on his behalf. We cried because of our human weakness. We did not know that the Lord would use this tragedy to transform lives and bring unconverted souls to His kingdom. Like Sarah, we thought this was an impossible task to deal with. However, during this crisis, we realized that all our impossibilities are God's opportunity to work miracles and alter events in our lives for His glory.

"Let us start a nightly conference call prayer line," Carol suggested. We all agreed to start the following night, which was Saturday night. That was the start of our "Family Power-Packed Prayer Line." This line continues to be a blessing to all who desire to participate by calling the line or sending a prayer request. At the beginning, it was simply "the prayer line." However, when I started to write this chapter, two times in a single week my brother Harold prayed the phrase, "family power-packed prayer line." The Holy Spirit said, "That is the topic for this chapter." He is still my Guide and Teacher.

We did not know how powerfully the Holy Spirit would work for us through this ministry, bringing healing, blessing, and comfort to hundreds of family members and friends. On the first Saturday night, over fifty family members agonized and pleaded with the Lord to heal Garfield, who was then just a young man.

The Scriptures declare: "Behold, I will bring it health and healing; I will heal them and reveal to them the abundance of peace and truth" (Jer. 33:6).

> **On the first Saturday night, over fifty family members agonized and pleaded with the Lord to heal Garfield, who was then just a young man.**

Jesus promised: "Again I say to you that if two of you agree on earth concerning anything that they ask, it will be done for them by My Father in heaven. For where two or three are gathered together in My name, I am there in the midst of them" (Matt. 18:19, 20).

Ellen White encouraged the use of united prayers. "We are encouraged to pray for success, with the divine assurance that our prayers will be heard and answered.... The promise is made on condition that the united prayers of the church [our family was the church] are offered, and in answer to these prayers there may be expected a power greater than that which comes in answer to private prayer. The power given will be proportionate to the unity of the members and their love for God and for one another" (Letter 32, 1903, in *Manuscript Releases*, vol. 9, p. 303).

Family members from Jamaica, Canada, New York, New Jersey, Florida, and Georgia engaged in an hour of power, united in prayer for Garfield's physical, spiritual, emotional, and financial healing. Our practice has been to pray from Sunday through Thursday, 9 pm to 10 pm or until the Holy Spirit stops us.

Friday night was reserved for the children from five to twelve years of age. They, along with their parents, were responsible for moderating their own prayer meeting. The children's prayer line continued for one year. The adult prayer line has continued beyond that period, although the numbers have decreased. Some family members have started their own prayer lines, increasing the blessings to others.

Garfield's crisis revolutionized our personal and family life. We prayed for the salvation of our children, especially those who have left their faith. We prayed for spiritual, emotional, physical, and financial breakthroughs and reconciliation of broken family relationships. The psalmist reminds us in Psalm 86:6, 7: "Give ear, O LORD, to my prayer; and attend to the voice of my supplications. In the day of my trouble I will call upon You, for You will answer me."

God answered our prayers in a marvelous way. Two weeks after the prayer line started, Garfield was scheduled for surgery. The Saturday night before the surgery, we had a seven-hour prayer vigil on the prayer line. Biblically the number "seven" represents perfection, and it is God's sign of divine worship, completeness, obedience, and rest. We stormed the gates of heaven on Garfield's behalf. We pleaded with God for perfect restoration and for complete healing and rest for this young man. Ellen White identified Christ as still being the Great Physician. Every suffering one may be taught that the Great Physician loves and cares for all His children and that He longs to heal them.

"All life-giving power is from Him. When one recovers from disease, it is God who restores him" (*The Ministry of Healing*, p. 113).

"He is our refuge in sickness as in health. 'Like as a father pitieth his children, so the Lord pitieth him that fear Him....' Psalm 103:13 ... '... He sendeth His word, and healeth them, and delivereth them from their destructions. ... God is just as willing to restore the sick to health now as when the Holy Spirit spoke these words through the psalmist. And Christ is the same compassionate physician now that He was during His earthly ministry. In Him there is healing balm for every disease, restoring power for every infirmity (*The Ministry of Healing*, pp. 225, 226).

We prayed earnestly that God would answer our prayers and heal Garfield. Our prayers focused on the doctors and surgeons, the nurses, the instruments, the hospital room, and anyone connected with his surgery. The surgery was scheduled to last an estimated seven hours. Miraculously, it took only three to four hours. That was the first answer to our prayers.

More than this, no cancer was found! The surgeons were puzzled and shocked.

The following is how Garfield recalled the conversation with his surgeons and doctors.

"The doctors said that they removed a benign tumor. They also removed a part of my colon to send for further biopsy. They were baffled because they were the ones who had confirmed the diagnosis by biopsy. They took pictures of my colon, and microscopically they did not find any cancer cells. They were mystified. They were determined to find the cancer. They sent part of the test to the United States for further analysis and diagnosis. The entire test came back negative. They were confounded because they had never experienced anything like this in their years of practice. I was their miracle patient, they said. My case was discussed at every staff meeting in the hospital."

After the surgery, a family member called to give us the answer God wanted us to hear. We rejoiced with inexpressible joy. We praised God for His miracle. On the prayer line that night we agreed with the psalmist when he shouted: "Bless the LORD, O my soul; and all that is within me, bless His holy name! Bless the LORD, O my soul, and forget not all His benefits: who forgives all your iniquities, who heals all your diseases, who redeems your life from destruction, who crowns you with loving kindness and tender mercies" (Ps. 103:1–4).

Jesus is still the Great Physician! Garfield is fully recovered and is praising God for the second chance that was given him of an additional eight years of life. He testifies:

> I continue to thank God for healing me. As often as I can, I share my testimony about my healing. The people who are most impacted are those who saw the dramatic weight loss I experienced in a short time. They thought I would die. Most attributed the severe weight loss to AIDS (Acquired Immunodeficiency Syndrome), the most severe phase of HIV infection, which attacks the body's immune system and leads to death if not treated. HIV is a disease of the immune system that destroys the (CD4) T lymphocytes of the immune system, leaving the body vulnerable to life-threatening infections and cancers.
>
> There was genuine curiosity about my recovery. I was told time and time again that the expectation was to hear that I had died. I lost more than fifty pounds within three months. I could not conceal the physical, emotional, and most of the spiritual pain I experienced during my trial.

The only comfort, peace, and joy was that my family line prayer members agonized and pleaded my case nightly before God, who told them to pray. He reminded them of His promise in Matthew 10:8: "Heal the sick, cleanse the leper, raise the dead. Freely you have received freely give." I am a recipient of that healing power.

Another miracle happened. Prior to my surgery, I was diagnosed with an irregular heartbeat. This is usually fatal if not treated before surgery. I had my surgery and survived. There is only one reason I am alive today: God cares and He hears. He answers prayers. I am growing stronger in the Lord, and the broken relationship with my daughter has been restored. I am praising and thanking God. My life is one miracle after another.

The Holy Spirit continues to use Garfield for His glory. The Spirit saw that, while we were praying fervently, another element of our prayer life was missing. It was something very special that would give us more power to pray and develop our faith in God.

After this, the Holy Spirit impressed Garfield one night while he was asleep with the message: "Your Bible is closed." The Spirit repeated the message twice. Garfield said that he did not understand the meaning of the statement for he had been reading his Bible. He relayed the information to the rest of us on the prayer line that night.

"Immediately, my aunt Phillippa said that the Holy Spirit was directing us to study the Bible on the prayer line."

That was the beginning of intense Bible study on the nightly prayer line.

Why is studying the Bible so very important? Paul answers in Hebrews 4:12: "For the word of God is living and powerful, and sharper than any two-edged sword, piercing even to the division of soul and spirit, and of joints and marrow, and is a discerner of the thoughts and intents of the heart."

Note Ellen White's instruction about the Bible. "The Bible should be made the foundation of study and of teaching. The essential knowledge is a knowledge of God and of Him whom He has sent. ... The whole Bible is a revelation of the glory of God in Christ. Received, believed, obeyed, it is the great instrumentality in the transformation of character. It is the grand stimulus, the constraining force, that quickens the physical, mental, and spiritual powers, and directs the life into right channels" (*The Ministry of Healing*, pp. 401, 458).

Tuesday nights we have designated for intensive Bible study, and these are conducted by the author. In our study, we have used the Amazing Facts study guides, the Voice of Prophecy study on Daniel, *The Power of Prayer* series. We have also studied several other topics. We are presently studying my very favorite topic of the Holy Spirit. We have read through the Bible twice. The Bible is the foundation of our study and teaching. Many lives have been transformed and reformed by studying the Word. Many members have expressed that they have heard some truths for the first time. Three accepted the Sabbath truth. We all agree that God's Word is truly a lamp unto our feet and a light to our path.

The prayer line has been a blessing to our family and friends. Here are testimonies from several of our members.

Harold's Testimony. (My youngest brother, the priest of the prayer line, is Garfield's father.) "God has done amazing things for my son because of our prayers. It is my determination to make this prayer line a part of my prayer life continually. It is the main connection to the powerhouse of the Holy Spirit where I get my daily supply of power. I depend on this prayer line. We pray daily for protection and ask the Holy Spirit not to let Satan rejoice over God's children. I recall this incident. The following day, after having had an intense and spirit-filled prayer line service, I went to work. I fell from the top to the bottom of a steep flight of stairs and hit my head. I was unconscious. No one was near me except the angels. They sprang into operation when they saw me lying there motionless. They protected me. I woke up. I knew that it was the prayer of protection that we pray every night that is the reason I am still alive. I get strength to cope spiritually, mentally, physically, and emotionally. I thank God for all my children. I can see His hands guiding them daily."

Marcia's Testimony. "I am a registered nurse working in home health. I minister to clients in their homes while performing my nursing duties. I met a very fragile young adult who was diagnosed with cancer. I invited her to join the prayer line. She accepted. Although she was very sick, she called the prayer line. As her love for the Lord grew and her faith increased, she became like Andrew, one of Jesus' disciples. Andrew brought other people whom he wanted to hear the good news of salvation through Jesus. She heard and accepted new truths about the Sabbath, the state of the dead, hell, and salvation through Jesus. She became a regular member of the prayer line. She invited her friends and family to join the prayer line, and they accepted. She was responsible for over ten friends and family members joining the prayer line. They were blessed. Her two sons, who are in middle school, also participated in the children's prayer line.

"The Holy Spirit developed a relationship between our families. One Thanksgiving weekend, this lady and her sons were invited to fellowship with us. It was a blessing when she met several other family members who had come from New York and Florida to Georgia for the Thanksgiving celebration.

"I was surprised to learn that my nephew attended the same middle school with her sons. They knew each other! They too could meet and share their experience about the children's prayer line.

"Shortly after that weekend, the lady became very sick. She lapsed into a coma and was placed on respiratory support. We had a seven-hour prayer vigil on her behalf. During the vigil, my aunt Phillippa said that, while she was praying, she saw four angels with fiery flames alighted in her room. She was calm and tranquil and very peaceful. We continued praying for her healing according to God's will. Not long afterward, she opened her eyes and said goodbye to the parents who had been constantly at her bedside.

"I am blessed to know that our family prayer line was and is still used as an outreach to encourage hurting and lost souls and to bring the good news of salvation to all who participate on the line. I know that I will see my patient, my friend on 'that great getting up morning.'"

Blessings from a nephew's perspective: Horace's Testimony. "The prayer line has certainly changed my life. I have become closer and more intimate with God through the work of the Holy Spirit in my life. I witnessed how the Holy Spirit worked through prayer and the power of God to heal my cousin of cancer. The nightly prayer meetings have held our families together and healed and restored broken relationships. Prayer has transformed hate into love and unforgiveness into forgiveness. Family members who had not spoken to each other for many years have been reconciled. We have prayed and asked the Holy Spirit to provide jobs for the jobless, hope for the hopeless, and companions for the lonely. He has answered our prayers. I have also observed that many unbelieving family members have been drawn closer to the Lord. I have heard testimonies from family members about how the Holy Spirit has worked miracles in their lives."

Carol's Testimony. "I held two mortgages with a commercial bank. I applied for modification to both loans. However, I noticed that only one was modified. I went to the bank and tried every possible means to have that loan modified. I was told it could not be modified. We continued to pray about the problem.

I returned several times. Finally, one manager told me that they could not modify a loan that cannot be found. I was mystified. *Why couldn't they find documents for a large loan?* I thought.

We continued to intercede passionately on the prayer line. We pleaded with the Holy Spirit to take charge and resolve this problem according to His will. One day I received an express mail from the bank. I was terrified. However, when I opened the mail, I shouted, 'Praise the Lord! Thank You, Jesus!' The letter stated that they had forgiven my debt. The loan will be written off and reported to all three credit bureaus as a debt 'PAID

IN FULL.' No negative report would be on my credit report. That night on the prayer line we screamed, 'Hallelujah! To God be the glory!' He has done great things because we prayed and believed His Word."

Richie's Testimony. (My sister Richie and her daughter Pat were blessed by the Lord to relocate from the busy streets of Brooklyn to a quaint, beautiful snowcapped town in upstate New York. This is her testimony about God's mercy and how the family prayer line brought her joy and peace and eternal salvation. Before she joined the prayer line, Satan terrified her and would have killed her before she could enjoy the blessing of living in the beautiful home the Lord has blessed and provided for her.) "The first year I moved to this house, I was crippled with fear. I was terrified of being in a big house alone during the day. I panicked when it snowed, thinking my daughter would get stuck in the snow on the highway. She had a three-hour commute to work as a school principal. I would call my sister Phillippa or my niece Marcia or Cynthia to pray with me. On Friday evenings, my sister Phillippa would call me and have worship with me. However, I was still fearful and hopeless. The first Thanksgiving in the new house, many of my relatives visited to share my blessings. The house was dedicated to the Lord. My brother Harold prayed a powerful prayer of protection for every window, door, and wall in the house. My fears and anxiety gradually went away.

"My greatest blessing happened when the prayer line started. I experienced tremendous satisfaction. My fears disappeared. It was unbelievable that I could connect and pray with so many family members. I had not heard from some for many years. The prayer line brought joy, peace, and, above all, truth, which allowed me to make the most important life-changing decision in accepting Jesus as my Lord and Savior and embracing the Seventh-day Adventist faith. Before the prayer line, I was not familiar with many Bible truths. After studying the Amazing Facts lessons on Daniel, new light was revealed to me. I am converted and ready for baptism as a commandment-keeping Seventh-day Adventist Christian. Satan meant Garfield's tragedy for evil; God meant it for good.

"I yearn for the prayer line daily. At nights, many family members are on. However, at noon, at least six members and friends, including myself, agonize for our children. My faith and my trust in God has increased. My prayer life is stronger as I pray for the salvation of my children and my grandchildren. They call me often and ask questions about their salvation. I am blessed that I can give a biblical answer and guide and instruct them.

"God truly answers prayers. My daughter needed a car. We prayed on the line. We asked God's guidance and favor. One Sunday evening, to satisfy me, we drove to a dealership near our house and went inside. Someone called from behind and asked, 'Can I help you? Can I help you?'

"'Yes,' I replied.

"'You are at the right place. The Lord sent you to me. I am the answer to your prayer. Have faith.'

"I was amazed with his introduction and his response. *Wow*, I thought to myself. He took down the necessary information. Then he went to speak with his boss and returned to say, 'A miracle happened; she will get her car.' There were two cars that my daughter liked. Both were available. She walked out with a signed document. The following day she picked up her new car.

"For a weak, timid person, my faith has grown tremendously. I have experienced the Holy Spirit in my life. Sometimes I encounter an overwhelming peace, love, and joy that comes by abiding in the Lord through prayer and studying the Word.

"The Holy Spirit has blessed me to be the one assigned to select the family of the month and the night they are to be prayed for. Each time I have selected someone, they have had a need for prayer for that night or that month. My faith has increased because of the work of the Holy Spirit in my life.

"Like the psalmist, I declare, 'I will lift up mine eyes unto the hills, from whence cometh my help. My help cometh from the LORD, which made heaven and earth. He will not suffer thy foot to be moved: he that keepeth thee will not slumber. Behold he that keepeth Israel shall neither slumber nor sleep. The LORD is thy keeper: the LORD is thy shade upon thy right hand. The sun shall not smite thee by day, nor the moon by night. The LORD shall preserve thee from all evil: he shall preserve thy soul. The LORD shall preserve thy going out and thy coming in from this time forth, and even for ever more.' (Psalm 121:1–8, KJV)."

Pauline's Testimony. "A car belonging to my son, Andre, who is a college student, was stolen. We prayed and asked the Holy Spirit to help him find the car. After two weeks, the police called. The car had been found without any damage. I also prayed for a car for myself. I received an unexpected check from my job and purchased a car. Praise God from whom all blessings flow!"

Olive's Testimony. "My son Mark was traveling from Atlanta to Jacksonville. He was driving at a normal speed, but his car flipped over three times. He sustained no injuries, while the car was written off on the spot. He returned home safely and did not receive any medical attention. Many years after that accident, he was physically fit to join the United States Navy. I am the leader for the midday prayer line. My commitment is to continue to pray for the protection and salvation of our children, our friend's children, and the children of the world."

Also, my daughter got married, and, after many years of trying to conceive, she had a miscarriage. She was devastated, thinking that she would not have any children. The family prayed and interceded passionately for her and her husband, asking God to bless her womb again. In their seventh year of marriage, the Lord answered their prayer. He blessed them with a healthy baby boy on the seventh day of the third month of that seventh year. He is the pride and joy of their heart. Thank God for His completing His promise, "Ask and it shall be given to you; seek and you shall find; knock and it shall be opened to you" (Matt. 7:7).

Sybil's Testimony. "I am one of the original prayer line members who prayed for Garfield that first night. I have participated on the prayer line for many years. I have been truly blessed by being in the presence of the Lord and worshiping with family and friends. I could not keep these blessings to myself. I invited some of my friends to participate. They too have been blessed. After a while, I became less involved. Sometimes I have been absent for months. I had no reason for not taking part. Satan had stepped in and blocked my vision. One night, I became ill, and the Holy Spirit urged me to call the line that night. I spoke in a very low voice. The members realized that I was sick. The following Saturday night, they held a seven-hour prayer vigil on my behalf, and I was healed. I have been on the prayer line since then and co-host the Thursday night service of praise and thanksgiving with my sister Pauline."

Paulene's Testimony. "I was invited to the prayer line by one of my dearest friends, Sybil. My daughter became very sick. This ministry has been a tremendous blessing. I later had a serious respiratory problem. I was in respiratory failure and developed a rapid heart rate. I could hardly speak in a complete sentence. The members thought that every breath I took would be my last. The prayer line interceded on my behalf. Today I am healed and blessed, and I am the Sunday night host. I have no respiratory problem."

Miss Walker's Testimony. "I am blessed to be a part of this wonderful ministry. I wait every noon and evening for the time to arrive to get on the line. I love the interaction and the encouraging testimonies from the members. I am blessed to be one of the 'soloists' on the line, singing the song of meditation before we pray. I joined the prayer line a year ago. My life has been changed by God's answers to prayer. My daughter lives in Jamaica. She lost her job and unsuccessfully sought employment for many months. Then she was diagnosed with a devastating illness and was hospitalized. The doctors estimated that she would be hospitalized for eight to ten weeks and that surgery was a strong possibility. Her health deteriorated and she became unresponsive. To complicate matters, there were no beds available in the intensive care unit where she needed to be.

Since I have been living in the United States, visiting family and friends would call me almost daily with depressing news, doubtful that my daughter would ever leave the hospital. At the time, I had my own health challenges and could not travel. My daughter's church family was not allowed to see her. The prayer line family started to intercede more fervently on her behalf, fasting for her and launching a seven-day daily prayer on her behalf to ask God for complete healing. Thanks and praise to God, after seventeen days of hospitalization without admission to the intensive care unit, she was discharged! She completed her recovery at home and started searching again for a job. She was offered one, accepted it, and the Monday that she started, she received another job offer for a position that was to start immediately. She decided to take the first offer. She and the prayer line family are thanking and praising God for His miracles."

Miss Irene's Testimony. "This has been a powerful blessing to me and my family. Lives have been changed, relationships have been restored. Prayers were made on behalf of relatives who needed jobs. God answered these prayers. I am blessed to be the Monday night host and one of the 'soloists.' This is the night we pray for our children—especially those who have left the church."

Sister Mackenzie's Testimony. "I praise the Lord that I became a part of this prayer line. A year after joining, I returned to the true church, the Seventh-day Adventist Church. Now I am a happy and proud member. I look forward every night to being on the prayer line."

Cynthia's Testimony. "I hurriedly closed the administrative offices at my church, having a very short time to get home before the school bus arrives with my elementary-age twins. I heard a strong impression telling me to 'go back to the church and pray.' I responded to the Holy Spirit, 'I can pray in the van.' I was already late leaving the office. I debated with the Holy Spirit. I knew that I would be very late for the arrival of the children if I returned to the sanctuary to pray. My young children would be standing outside without any communication from their mother and would probably be very worried.

"I obeyed the Holy Spirit. I returned to the sanctuary and prayed for my cousin who was scheduled to have surgery that morning. I learned that night on the prayer line that the surgery had been rescheduled for the afternoon, the very time the Holy Spirit insisted that I return to the sanctuary and pray. God answered my prayer. The surgery was successful because I was obedient and listened to the instructions of the Holy Spirit to return to the sanctuary and pray. When I arrived home, I found that the bus was unusually late, so I was waiting when the twins arrived home.

"My encouragement to everyone is to start a family prayer line. Be blessed."

A former Seventh-day Adventist was searching to reconnect with her faith. Her sister, who lives in another state, told her about the prayer line. She called and was blessed to learn that the Holy Spirit uses our prayer line to bless strangers as well as our family. After studying for a year, she committed her life to the Lord and was re-baptized.

She became like the Samaritan woman whom Jesus met at the well and offered eternal life. When she accepted, she immediately went to her village and told the residents, "Come, see a Man who told me all things that I ever did. Could this be the Christ?" (John 4:29). In a similar way, the Lord entrusted this reconnected former Adventist lady with a ministry to seek out former Seventh-day Adventists. Several of these have attended church with her and have followed up with Bible studies. Her children and grandchildren have also been blessed, and her grandchildren attend church with her, participating in the Adventurers Club. Her life and her home have been transformed!

CHAPTER 11

Rejoice with Me!

> Behold, I give you the authority to trample on serpents and scorpions, and over all the power of the enemy, and nothing shall by any means hurt you. Nevertheless do not rejoice in this, that the spirits are subject to you, but rather rejoice because your names are written in heaven.
> —Luke 10:19, 20

I am humbled and awestruck with the God of the universe, "For the eyes of the LORD run to and fro throughout the whole earth, to show Himself strong on behalf of those whose heart is loyal to Him" (2 Chron. 16:9). I am blessed that He chose me to be one of His loyal servants. Since He called me into ministry, He has guided and instructed me with promises from the Scriptures. These promises have made a profound impact in my life, changing me from a nominal Christian to a Christ-centered practicing Christian. Here are a few of those promises:

"You will keep him in perfect peace, whose mind is stayed on You, because he trusts in You" (Isa. 26:3).

"O LORD, You are my God. I will exalt You, I will praise Your name, for You have done wonderful things; Your counsels of old are faithfulness and truth" (Isa. 25:1).

"The LORD will guide you continually, and satisfy your soul in drought, and strengthen your bones; you shall be like a watered garden, and like a spring of water, whose waters do not fail" (Isa. 58:11).

"I indeed baptize you with water unto repentance, but He who is coming after me is mightier than I, whose sandal I am not worthy to carry. He will baptize you with the Holy Spirit and fire" (Matt. 3:11).

I use these promises as a testimony that the Bible is real. God is real. Jesus and the Holy Spirit are real. They worked together to make this spiritual journey a success, one in which I can rejoice that I have finally found Jesus as my Lord and Savior and King of kings because Jesus declared to me concerning the Holy Spirit: "However, when He, the Spirit of truth, has come, He will guide you into all truth; for He will not speak on His own authority, but whatever He hears He will speak; and He will tell you things to come" (John 16:3).

Power Through the Word

One of Jesus' greatest insights for me is found in John 15:16: "You did not choose Me, but I chose you and appointed you that you should go and bear fruit, and that your fruit should remain, that whatever you ask the Father in My name He may give you."

How would I bear fruit for the Lord? What method would He use to teach me to bear fruit for Him? What is the relationship between bearing fruit, the Holy Spirit, and rejoicing in the Lord?

The answers to these questions are found in John 15:1–8 (KJV): "I am the true vine, and my Father is the husbandman. Every branch in me that beareth not fruit he taketh away: and every branch that beareth fruit, he purgeth it, that it may bring forth more fruit. Now ye are clean through the word which I have spoken unto you. Abide in me, and I in you. As the branch cannot bear fruit of itself, except it abide in the vine; no more can ye, except ye abide in me. I am the vine, ye are the branches: He that abideth in me, and I in Him, the same bringeth forth much fruit: for without me ye can do nothing. If a man abide not in me, he is cast forth as a branch, and is withered; and men gather them, and cast them into the fire, and they are burned. If ye abide in me, and my words abide in you, ye shall ask what ye will, and it shall be done unto you. Herein is my Father glorified, that ye bear much fruit; so shall ye be my disciples."

This illustration taught me a very important biblical truth about bearing fruit. The first truth and main principle that it taught me is: "Abide in Me."

How is "abiding" in Christ accomplished? Can I abide in Christ by doing good works such as attending church and holding office at church? While these things might be an indication that I want to abide in Christ, they are not evidence that I am abiding.

Ellen White defines how the Christian abides in Christ.

> "Herein is My Father glorified," said Jesus, "that ye bear much fruit." God desires to manifest through you the holiness, the benevolence, the compassion of His own character. Yet the Saviour does not bid the disciples labor to bear fruit. He tells them to abide in Him. "If ye abide in Me," He says, "and My words abide in you, ye shall ask what ye will, and it shall be done unto you." It is through the word that Christ abides in His followers. This is the same vital union that is represented by eating His flesh and drinking His blood. The words of Christ are spirit and life. Receiving them, you receive the life of the Vine. You live "by every word that proceedeth out of the mouth of God." Matthew 4:4. The life of Christ in you produces the same fruits as in Him. Living in Christ, adhering to Christ, supported by Christ, drawing nourishment from Christ, you bear fruit after the similitude of Christ. (*The Desire of Ages*, p. 677)

The word of God was revealed to me when I prayed and asked the Lord for clear instructions on the journey. Prayer was the channel of communication between God and my soul. The Scriptures teach us to "pray without ceasing" (1 Thess. 5:17). As I prayed and listened to the Holy Spirit, I was able to endure my trials and tribulations through the Scriptures that God gave me. The psalmist exclaimed: "Your word is a lamp to my feet and a light to my path" (Ps. 119:105).

That light guided me through the darkest hours when I had tried on my own but was not able to restore the broken relationship with the only child the Lord had blessed me with. The light directed my path in understanding the frustration experienced by a teen who felt rejected by her friends, her family, and especially her parents. As I read the Bible I was favored by the Holy Spirit because I followed the light I received, and my heart was opened to greater light and greater truths. Jesus declared, "I am the light of the world. He who follows Me shall not walk in darkness, but have the light of life" (John 8:12).

That light allowed me to understand the great conflict between God and Satan. My daughter and I were caught in this battle. However, although we walked "through the valley of the shadow of death" (Ps. 23:4), I feared no evil, for God was with us. His Word was sure. He told me through the message that He gave Joshua, "Have I not commanded you? Be strong and of good courage; do not be afraid, nor be dismayed, for the LORD your God is with you wherever you go" (Joshua 1:9). It was very reassuring to me that the Lord promised that I would always be in His presence where there "is fullness of joy" (Ps. 16:11).

I took His wise counsel. I studied the word with passion and fervency. I meditated upon the Word. I followed the psalmist's counsel, "I will meditate on Your precepts, and contemplate Your ways. I will delight myself in Your statutes; I will not forget Your word" (Ps. 119:15, 16). "When I remember You on my bed, I meditate on You in the night watches" (Ps. 63:6).

Ellen White described how the Scriptures were helpful to Jesus: "He studied the word of God, and His hours of greatest happiness were found when He could turn aside from the scene of His labors ... to hold communion with God ... The early morning often found Him in some secluded place, meditating, searching the Scriptures, or in prayer. With the voice of singing He welcomed the morning light. With songs of thanksgiving He cheered His hours of labor and brought heaven's gladness to the toilworn and disheartened" (*The Ministry of Healing*, p. 52).

I followed Jesus' example. While reading the Scriptures, the Lord instructed me to prayerfully study Hebrews 4:12—"For the word of God is living and powerful, and sharper than any two-edged sword, piercing even to the division of soul and spirit, and of joints and marrow, and is a discerner of the thoughts and intents of the heart." *The Seventh-day Adventist Bible Commentary*, vol. 7, p. 424–425, enlightened me on its meaning, application, and implications in my life.

"**Word.** Gr. *logos* (see on John 1:1). In the context the 'word' here referred to is the 'word' that was 'preached' both to ancient Israel and to Christians." I was amazed how the Holy Spirit revealed this scripture verse to me while I prayed. It was the key scripture at a prayer conference I attended shortly after the revelation. The presenter expounded on this verse. I was blessed.

"**Quick.** That is, 'living.' It takes a living and active force to create in man a new heart and renew a right spirit within him (cf. Ps. 51:10). The 'word' of God is living, and imparts life. Thus it was in the work of creation (Ps. 33:6, 9) and thus it is in the re-creation of the image of God in the soul of man." It was the "living word" of God that imparted a new life to me. I loved my daughter unconditionally—even when she vowed that "we would never have a relationship." In her darkness, she did not know the power of God's Word. It is the "living word" that imparted life to my child and transformed her. We are experiencing the best relationship we have ever had.

"***Powerful.*** Gr. *energēs*, 'effective,' 'active,' 'powerful' (cf. on 1 Cor. 12:6). Our word 'energy' is derived from *energēs*. There is power in God's 'word' to transform sinners into saints." This power is working in my life and in my daughter's life. The awesome Spirit filled the void that had engulfed us, and He set us free. This transformation shows the power of the Word to change sinners.

"*Discerner.* Gr. *kritikos,* 'able to discern,' 'able to judge,' 'able to discriminate,' that is, possessed of the quality of discernment or discrimination. The English word 'critic' is derived from *kritikos.* By a favorable response to the impression made upon the conscience by God's 'word' the sincere Christian avoids falling into 'unbelief,' ceases from 'his own works,' and enters into God's 'rest' (vs. 6, 10, 11; cf. ch. 3:10, 12)."

When my daughter returned home, I was ashamed and embarrassed that she had not fulfilled my dream of becoming "my daughter the doctor." I wanted to fix the situation instantly and restore her life. However, I had to cease from "my own works" and allow the Holy Spirit to take control. I could "discern" Satan's attacks and tactics in our lives as I studied the Scriptures and prayed. I became less critical and surrendered my life to God. I watched as the Holy Spirit worked one miracle after another in our lives.

"**Thoughts and intents.** Or, 'thoughts and motives,' 'thoughts and intentions' (RSV). Like a sharp blade separating 'joints' from 'marrow,' the clear principles of the 'word of God' discern between good and evil thoughts, right and wrong motives." When the trials and sufferings intensified, I was tempted to say unkind, caustic and bitter words to my child. The Spirit encouraged me to "be still" and "do not say a word to her." I listened to that inner voice. It was the voice of reason, the Holy Spirit. He allowed me to determine the motive and intent of my response to her arguments. My motives at the time were anger, bitterness, and resentment. As I studied the Scriptures, my motives changed, becoming redemptive and pure. "Blessed are the pure in heart for they shall see God" (Matt. 5:8).

Rejoice with me that abiding in the Word is transformative and redemptive. "Rejoice and again I say rejoice."

Another principle of bearing fruit and rejoicing in the Lord is accepting the truth that Jesus declared in saying, "I am the Vine, ye are the branches."

I asked myself the question, "What is the relationship between the Vine and the branch?"

"How can the branch rejoice?" Ellen White answered the question. "I am the Vine, ye are the branches," Christ said to His disciples. Though He was about to be removed from them, their spiritual union with Him was to be unchanged. The connection of the branch with the vine, He said, represents the relation you are to sustain to Me. The scion is engrafted into the living vine, and fiber by fiber, vein by vein, it grows into the vine stock. The life of the vine becomes the life of the branch. So the soul dead in trespasses and sins receives life through connection with Christ. By faith in Him as a personal Saviour the union is formed. The sinner unites his weakness to Christ's strength, his emptiness to Christ's fullness, his frailty to Christ's enduring might. Then he has the mind of Christ. The humanity of Christ has touched our humanity, and our humanity has touched divinity. Thus through the agency of the Holy Spirit man becomes a partaker of the divine nature. He is accepted in the Beloved. (*The Desire of Ages*, p. 611).

I struggled to understand the broken relationship between my daughter and me, and I realized that our souls were dead in trespasses and sin. We needed to receive life through connecting with Christ. I needed to be connected to the Vine so that my life would become the vine's life and the vine's life would become mine. I united my weakness, anger, bitter resentment, and hatred with His strength, love, joy, peace, meekness, temperance, and longsuffering. I united the emptiness of my longing to be loved by my only child with Christ's fullness. His divinity touched us. He accepted us as branches so that we could maintain a connection with Him.

I continued abiding in Christ, by studying the Bible and praying. I recognized that, once the union with Christ is formed, it must be maintained because "the branch cannot bear fruit of itself" (John 15:4). The branch is part of the living vine. If separated from the vine, the branch cannot live. I purposed in my heart to continue abiding in Christ. "Abiding in Christ means a constant receiving of His Spirit, a life unreserved surrender to His service" (*The Desire of Ages*, p. 676). I prayed and asked for a double portion of His Holy Spirit so that my life would reflect His love to my daughter and to others.

Jesus pronounced another principle in rejoicing and bearing fruit:

> "And every branch that beareth fruit, He purgeth [pruneth] it, that it may bring forth more fruit." From the chosen twelve who had followed Jesus, one as a withered branch was about to be taken away; the rest were to pass under the pruning knife of bitter trial. Jesus with solemn tenderness explained the purpose of the husbandman. The pruning will cause pain, but it is the Father who applies the knife. He works with no wanton hand or indifferent heart. There are branches trailing upon the ground; these must be cut loose from the earthly supports to which their tendrils are fastening. They are to reach heavenward, and find their support in God. The excessive foliage that draws away the life current from the fruit must be pruned off. The overgrowth must be cut out, to give room for the healing beams of the Sun of Righteousness. The husbandman prunes away the harmful growth, that the fruit may be richer and more abundant. (*The Desire of Ages*, p. 612)

Although I did not pass through trials as severe as those of the apostles, nevertheless, my trials were brutal. Bitterest of all was the fact that my only child had rejected me and her faith. The husbandman used this experience to cut away the harmful growth in my life so that I could bear fruit for Him. As I reflected on the pruning, the Holy Spirit revealed to me that I had put my daughter on a pedestal. Although I was attending church, I was a Christian in name but not in practice. Secondly, He showed me that my daughter had become my god, violating the command, "You shall have no other gods before Me" (Exod. 20:3), which God gave the children of Israel after they left Egypt where they had lost a knowledge of the true God.

Many years prior, God brought me out of "Egypt" where I had lost sight of the true and living God. Liberated, I accepted my Redeemer. His expectation was that I would abide in Him and bear much fruit for His kingdom. Nonetheless, I unintentionally began worshipping my daughter, her academic achievement and her musical talent from her first piano recital at age six onward. The possibility that she would become a physician blurred my true relationship with and genuine worship of the Lord. The excessive foliage of adoring my child weakened my connection with the Lord. When it was pruned away, growth from the Sun of Righteousness became more evident in my life.

Although my child is not a physician, I would not change for anything the years of "pruning" that I went through to "bear fruit." Looking back, those were the most exciting Spirit-filled years of my life. The ministry of the Holy Spirit in my life was one of the most transformative lessons I learned during that "season of pruning." Abiding in Christ is a gift through the power of the Holy Spirit.

In *The Coming of the Comforter*, pages 53 and 54, LeRoy E. Froom lists the Holy Spirit's five-fold office. I will use the first three of these to demonstrate how the Holy Spirit was real in teaching me how to *abide* and rejoice in Christ.

"1. He first reveals Christ as an abiding presence." "Better than His bodily presence during the Christian era, would be His abiding through the Spirit within His followers.... *'Henceforth through the Spirit, Christ was* *to abide continually in the hearts of His children. Their union with Him was closer than when He was personally with them.* The light, and love, and power of the indwelling Christ shone through them, so that men, beholding, "marveled; and they took knowledge of them, that they had been with Jesus."' —*'Steps to Christ,'* pp. 74, 75, pocket edition" (*The Coming of the Comforter,* p. 55). I marveled that my daughter observed that I had stopped arguing with her when she was angry. Instead, I responded to her with kind words or a hug. Thanks to the abiding Holy Spirit in me who instructed me, "Do not say a word when there is an argument," she stopped yelling and arguing when I stopped responding. This strategy was the turning point of our relationship.

"**2. He reveals God's truth, making it a reality in the innermost being.**" "'The Comforter is called "the Spirit of truth." His work is to define and maintain the truth. He first dwells in the heart as the Spirit of truth, and thus He becomes the Comforter. There is comfort and peace in the truth, but no real peace or comfort can be found in falsehood.' —*'The Desire of Ages,'* p. 671" (*The Coming of the Comforter,* p. 59). The truth He revealed to me was that I was incapable of restoring the broken relationship with my daughter without the help of the Holy Spirit. Satan lied, telling me that, if I tried hard enough, I would be able to restore the relationship. I had no peace when I held onto that falsehood. The truth of relying on the Holy Spirit brought unspeakable joy and comfort to a hurting, grieving mother.

"**3. He is intrusted to bring holiness to man.**" "'The Holy Spirit seeks to abide in each soul. ... The good work begun will be finished; the holy thoughts, heavenly affections, and Christlike actions will take the place of impure thoughts, perverse sentiments, and rebellious acts.' —*'Counsels on Health,'* p. 561" (*The Coming of the Comforter,* p. 57). The Holy Spirit is guiding my life. The good work was begun in my life as He replaced impure thoughts with pure ones and the mean and vicious actions toward my child went away.

In understanding the power of the Holy Spirit, I studied the Scriptures and discovered that the one prerequisite to receiving the Holy Spirit is to ask for Him. Luke 11:13 states, "If you then, being evil, know how to give good gifts to your children, how much more will your heavenly Father give the Holy Spirit to those who ask Him!" I prayed for a double portion of the Holy Spirit in my life and in my daughter's life. I asked for His abiding presence to dwell in me so that my daughter could see Christ in me.

Observe Froom's comments on this point: "Through the ages past the Holy Spirit had been *with* men, but from Pentecost forward God's purpose was that He 'shall be in you.' This is to be the sacred reality. The world receives Him not because it sees Him not. The world's devotion is to the visible, the material. But the Christian is to realize the personal occupancy and the indwelling of God the Spirit" (*The Coming of the Comforter*, p. 56).

Could anyone see the indwelling of the Spirit in me? Was fruit bearing evident in me? I tested the idea on my only child who had told me, after she was expelled from the university, "I will never have a relationship with you." Years after praying for the Holy Spirit to abide in me and transform my life, I asked her, "Have you seen a change in me?"

"Mom, since you started the prayer ministry, you are a different person. You mean everything to me. You are my blessing and my love. Thank you for all that you do for me." I was spellbound. The Holy Spirit was dwelling in us. Luke records in Acts 1:8: "But you shall receive power when the Holy Spirit has come upon you; and you shall be witnesses to Me in Jerusalem [my home], and in all Judea and Samaria, and to the end of the earth." I thank God for the indwelling presence of God the Spirit in my life, and I thank Him that the one with whom I daily interact witnessed that transformation.

My daughter's life has been transformed. It is evident that God the Spirit is working in her life. Acts 2:38, 39 declares: "Then Peter said to them, "Repent, and let every one of you be baptized in the name of Jesus Christ for the remission of sins; and you shall receive the gift of the Holy Spirit. For the promise is to you and to your children, and to all who afar off."

My daughter was still "afar off." Yet, since the promise of the Holy Spirit was for me and for my child, could anyone see the Holy Spirit in her? Indeed they could. Several of her friends requested that she ask me to pray for them. Her best friend called her saying, "Please put my daughter and her father on your prayer list. We are divorced. He is moving to a different state. Please pray that he will continue to have a relationship with her. I presented the request to the prayer line. I continued to pray passionately for the family. I identified with this young mother, for my daughter did not have a good relationship with her father. I witnessed firsthand the consequences of a broken father-daughter relationship. Thank God for the Holy Spirit's healing power and the gift of reconciliation in their lives.

I am rejoicing because of the Lord's directing of my steps on this long journey concerning the power of prayer. Through it, I have come to understand the transformative power of the Holy Spirit. I rejoice in the many bright spots on this journey. The Scriptures and the inspired writings of Ellen White have been the brightest of these. The Scriptures have come alive and very real to me as God the Spirit has revealed Jesus and the Father to me. I have marveled how God's promises have strengthened my faith in His words and brought healing and reconciliation to my daughter and me. My heart is overwhelmed by the power of the Holy Spirit.

It has been very much like that which Ellen White described: "Have there not been some bright spots in your experience? Have you not had some precious seasons when your heart throbbed with joy in response to the Spirit of God? When you look back into the chapters of your life experience do you not find some pleasant pages? Are not God's promises, like the fragrant flowers, growing beside your path on every hand? Will you not let their beauty and sweetness fill your heart with joy?" (*Steps to Christ*, p. 117).

God's promises are indeed like fragrant flowers growing beside our paths. The Lord has fulfilled His promises in our lives and will continue to do so until we meet Him in the sky. In Jeremiah 30:17 He fulfilled that promise, " I will restore health to you and heal your wounds. Our wounds are healed. We are experiencing "our best" mother daughter relationship.

He has restored the wasted years of her life. "I will restore to you the years that the swarming locust has eaten. "Joel 2:25. My daughter graduated from a prestigious university with a BSN degree. She was inducted into the Honor Society of Nursing- Sigma Theta Tau International as a member of Chi Beta Chapter. She was encouraged to apply for a nursing position in the "Scholars" program at one of the hospital she did a clinical assignment.

I rejoice because God has restored our damaged souls. David says in Psalm 23:3 He restores my soul: He leads me in the path of righteousness. Whenever she calls and ask me to pray for her "I pray with her." Rejoice with me because we serve an awesome prayer answering God.

As I close, be blessed with these promises.

"Rejoice in the Lord alway; and again I say, Rejoice" (Phil. 4:4, KJV).

"Rejoice always" (1 Thess. 5:16).

"I rejoice at Your word as one who finds great treasure" (Ps. 119:162).

"And the disciples were filled with joy and with the Holy Spirit" (Acts 13:52).

"I will greatly rejoice in the LORD, my soul shall be joyful in my God; for He has clothed me with the garments of salvation, He has covered me with the robe of righteousness, as a bridegroom decks himself with ornaments, and as a bride adorns herself with her jewels" (Isa. 61:10).

"And when he comes home, he calls together his friends and neighbors, saying to them, 'Rejoice with me, for I have found my sheep which was lost!'" (Luke 15:6).

"I say to you that likewise there will be more joy in heaven over one sinner who repents than over ninety-nine just persons who need no repentance" (Luke 15:7).

"Or what woman, having ten silver coins, if she loses one coin, does not light a lamp, sweep the house, and search carefully until she finds it? And when she has found it, she calls her friends and neighbors together, saying, 'Rejoice with me, for I have found the piece which I lost!'" (Luke 15:8, 9). (I can say, Rejoice with *me*, for I have found my *daughter*, and we are experiencing the best relationship of our lives.)

"Nevertheless do not rejoice in this, that the spirits are subject to you, but rather rejoice because your names are written in heaven" (Luke 10:20). (Amen, and again I say, Amen!)

Bibliography

Froom, LeRoy E. *The Coming of the Comforter*. Hagerstown, MD: Review and Herald Publishing Association, 1999.

Review and Herald, Oct. 7, 1890.

Signs of the Times, Dec. 6, 1883.

White, Ellen G. *The Acts of the Apostles*. Mountain View, CA: Pacific Press Publishing Association, 1911.

White, Ellen G. *The Adventist Home*. Hagerstown, MD: Review and Herald Publishing Association, 1952.

White, Ellen G. *Child Guidance*. Washington, DC: Review and Herald Publishing Association, 1954.

White, Ellen G. *Christ's Object Lessons*. Washington, DC: Review and Herald Publishing Association, 1900.

White, Ellen G. *Christian Service*. Washington, DC: Review and Herald Publishing Association, 1925.

White, Ellen G. *Conflict and Courage*. Washington, DC: Review and Herald Publishing Association, 1970.

White, Ellen G. *The Desire of Ages*. Mountain View, CA: Pacific Press Publishing Association, 1898.

White, Ellen G. *Education*. Mountain View, CA: Pacific Press Publishing Association, 1903.

White, Ellen G. *God's Amazing Grace*. Washington, DC: Review and Herald Publishing Association, 1973.

White, Ellen G. *Gospel Workers*. Washington, DC: Review and Herald Publishing Association, 1915.

White, Ellen G. *The Great Controversy*. Mountain View, CA: Pacific Press Publishing Association, 1911.

White, Ellen G. *In Heavenly Places*. Washington, DC: Review and Herald Publishing Association, 1967.

White, Ellen G. *Manuscript Releases*. Vol. 3. Silver Spring, MD: Ellen G. White Estate, 1990.

White, Ellen G. *The Ministry of Healing*. Mountain View, CA: Pacific Press Publishing Association, 1905.

White, Ellen G. *Our High Calling*. Washington, DC: Review and Herald Publishing Association, 1961.

White, Ellen G. *Patriarchs and Prophets*. Washington, DC: Review and Herald Publishing Association, 1890.

White, Ellen G. *Prayer*. Nampa, ID: Pacific Press Publishing Association, 2002.

White, Ellen G. *Prophets and Kings*. Mountain View, CA: Pacific Press Publishing Association, 1917.

White, Ellen G. *Selected Messages*. Book 1. Washington, DC: Review and Herald Publishing Association, 1958.

White, Ellen G. *Selected Messages*. Book 2. Washington, DC: Review and Herald Publishing Association, 1958.

White, Ellen G. *The SDA Bible Commentary*. Vol. 3. Washington, DC: Review and Herald Publishing Association, 1954.

White, Ellen G. *The SDA Bible Commentary*. Vol. 4. Washington, DC: Review and Herald Publishing Association, 1955.

White, Ellen G. *The SDA Bible Commentary*. Vol. 7. Washington, DC: Review and Herald Publishing Association, 1957.

White, Ellen G. *Sons and Daughters of God*. Washington, DC: Review and Herald Publishing Association, 1955.

White, Ellen G. *Testimonies for the Church*. Vol. 2. Mountain View, CA: Pacific Press Publishing Association, 1871.

White, Ellen G. *Testimonies for the Church*. Vol. 4. Mountain View, CA: Pacific Press Publishing Association, 1881.

White, Ellen G. *Testimonies for the Church*. Vol. 5. Mountain View, CA: Pacific Press Publishing Association, 1889.

White, Ellen G. *Testimonies for the Church*. Vol. 6. Mountain View, CA: Pacific Press Publishing Association, 1901.

White, Ellen G. *Thoughts from the Mount of Blessing*. Mountain View, CA: Pacific Press Publishing Association, 1896.

Find Peace, Power, and Purpose for Your Life!

amazingfacts.org

Enroll in our FREE online Bible study course and discover:

- What happens after death
- The way to better health
- How to save your marriage
- The surprising news about hell
- Why the Bible is relevant today
- The "mark of the beast"
- Who really gets "left behind"
- ... and much more!

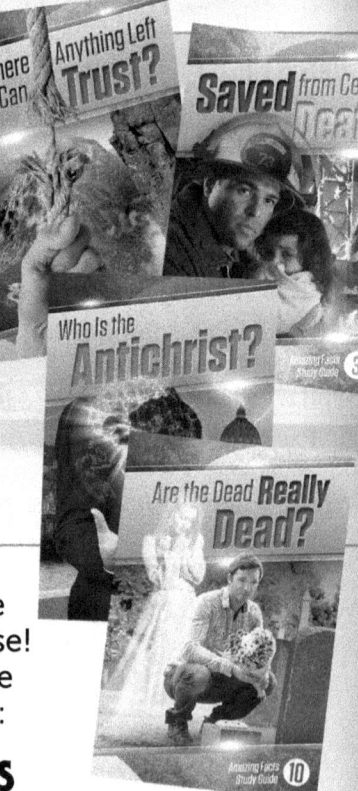

Or enroll in the postal mail course! Send your name and address to:

AMAZING FACTS

P.O. Box 909
Roseville, CA 95678

27 full-color, illustrated, Scripture-packed, easy-to-understand lessons!

TEACH Services, Inc.
P U B L I S H I N G
www.TEACHServices.com • (800) 367-1844

We invite you to view the complete
selection of titles we publish at:
www.TEACHServices.com

We encourage you to write us
with your thoughts about this,
or any other book we publish at:
info@TEACHServices.com

TEACH Services' titles may be purchased in
bulk quantities for educational, fund-raising,
business, or promotional use.
bulksales@TEACHServices.com

Finally, if you are interested in seeing
your own book in print, please contact us at:
publishing@TEACHServices.com

We are happy to review your manuscript at no charge.

www.ingramcontent.com/pod-product-compliance
Lightning Source LLC
Chambersburg PA
CBHW070540170426
43200CB00011B/2495